Doctrine and Experience

Doctrine and Experience

Caught in the Crossfire of Evangelical Spiritualities

Christopher C. Zito

Foreword by Ronald T. Michener

WIPF & STOCK · Eugene, Oregon

DOCTRINE AND EXPERIENCE
Caught in the Crossfire of Evangelical Spiritualities

Copyright © 2016 Christopher C. Zito. All rights reserved. Except for brief quotations in critical publications or reviews, no part of this book may be reproduced in any manner without prior written permission from the publisher. Write: Permissions, Wipf and Stock Publishers, 199 W. 8th Ave., Suite 3, Eugene, OR 97401.

Wipf & Stock
An Imprint of Wipf and Stock Publishers
199 W. 8th Ave., Suite 3
Eugene, OR 97401

www.wipfandstock.com

PAPERBACK ISBN: 978-1-4982-8119-5
HARDCOVER ISBN: 978-1-4982-8121-8
EBOOK ISBN: 978-1-4982-8120-1

Manufactured in the U.S.A.   06/24/2016

I dedicate this work to my wife Virginie, who has endured countless sacrifices throughout the years so I might pursue the studies and ministries that have allowed me to write the book in hand. If there will be any eternal prizes for my efforts, she will surely share in them.

Thank you.

"[J]ust when a person feels at home with a particular doctrine, experience may tap on the door of belief or vice versa and the conversation between doctrine and experience begins again."

—Karen E. Smith, *Christian Spirituality*, 10-11

Contents

Foreword Ronald T. Michener | ix
Preface | xiii

Introduction | 1
The Situation Today: The "Spiritualization" of Evangelicalism
Definitions and Objectives
Method

Chapter 1
Doctrinalism and Experientialism in the Evangelical Tradition | 9
Scholasticism, Puritanism, and Pietism
Revivalism and Princeton Theology
The Holiness Movement, Liberalism, and Fundamentalism
Neo-orthodoxy and Pentecostalism
(Neo-)Evangelicalism
The Charismatic Movement
Postscript: How History Humbles Us

Chapter 2
Bibliolatry: Making Idols of the Words of God | 41
Introduction to Bibliolatry
"Word of God" and the Bible
The Intellect, Spirituality, and Bible Facts
Bibliolatry and the Spirituality of the Bible
Bibliolatry, *Sola Scriptura*, and the Lordship of the Holy Spirit
Concluding Thoughts

Chapter 3
Pneumatolatry: Making an Idol of the Spirit of God | 76
    Introduction to Pneumatolatry
    The Order of Worship of the Triune God
    Put Up or Shut Up
    Everyone Who Asks Receives
    Embodying Spirituality in Imitation of Christ
    Concluding Thoughts

Chapter 4
Spirituality Caught in the Crossfire of Doctrine and Experience | 109
    Introduction
    Spirituality in the Church and Beyond
    The Turn towards the Inner Life in Evangelical Spiritualities
    An Embodied Spirituality of the Cross

Bibliography | 133
Index | 143

Foreword

Whatever it means to be an "evangelical," it clearly involves an intentional commitment to Bible-focused doctrine and a conversionist personal experience. Granted, the concept is much more complicated than this, but any attempt to define the term must not exclude these two essential ingredients. However, when these ingredients are mixed, the recipe becomes complex. Some favor the taste of vital truth in doctrinal expressions over fleeting emotive experientialism; others savor the vibrancy of the Spirit's work in human affections over the supposedly stale propositions of dogma. To take a preference one way or the other creates a climate of what Chris Zito calls, per the subtitle of this book, a "crossfire of evangelical spiritualities." Most would agree, of course, that we need both. We require doctrinal rigor according to the teachings of the Bible, and we desire changed lives (including our emotions and personal experiences) that are sensitive to the leading of the Holy Spirit. That is, we must apply doctrine to worship and everyday practices of faith. Chris wants us to eat the doctrinal cake, but he wants to taste its fruits through our lived faith and experience. As he deftly warns in this book, neither doctrine nor experience must be exaggerated at the expense of the other. If so, the recipe is spoiled and idolatry creeps in. One version of idolatry Chris describes is bibliolatry, where one's relationship with the words on the page of the Bible becomes the substitute for a vibrant relationship with the living God. The other Chris calls "pneumatolatry," where experiential encounters with the Holy Spirit take priority over the Bible. Of course, both tendencies are easy to find in the morass of contemporary Christian literature and within a variety of Christian movements.

Foreword

However, this book is not simply about warnings against extremes to achieve a balanced evangelical spirituality. Chris offers us a feast of renewed reflections on how, in the first place, our view of spirituality itself situates, colors, and shapes the way we end up manifesting that spirituality via one extreme or the other. In order to navigate through the unhealthy divide between doctrine and Spirit, Chris helps us retrace our evangelical historical steps to track down where and why we ended up with this chasm. Certainly, we cannot escape our backgrounds and contexts; they provide a lens through which we view and seek to understand the context of our spirituality. At the same time, we must learn and grow from our mistakes as we engage with diverse perspectives in the body of Christ. Chris argues for a robust, embodied spirituality that demands both mind and body as well as doctrine and experience should work together in profoundly authentic Christian living to manifest the living Spirit of God, who manifests and mediates the presence of the living, incarnate Jesus.

Doctrine matters, and so does the Spirit's guidance. Evangelical theologians and philosophers have struggled to articulate how these two are intertwined and in constant dialogue. In recent years, evangelical theologian Kevin Vanhoozer has suggested that we are performers of Christian doctrine, and the Spirit guides us in that performance through the script of Scripture. Philosopher James K. A. Smith has argued that we are embedded participants in embodied liturgical practices that shape our doctrine. A thick view of the human person in all his or her complexities must affirm both: our practices shape our doctrine, and our doctrine shapes our Christian practices. True Christian spirituality must also recognize that human bodies are indeed "spiritual" bodies, bodies that think and act in a real, physical world—bodies that participate in God's Spirit-infused creation. Chris promotes a spirituality that refuses the dichotomy between logic and affections. But he does not merely take a bit of logical doctrine and a sampling of affection and line them up as different aspects of the human person. Instead, he sees both doctrine and experience as integrated characteristics of evangelical spirituality, together manifesting the Spirit's guidance in worship and Christian discipleship.

I have appreciated Chris' clear thinking and astute scholarship through the years as I have had the opportunity to guide him in his theological studies, to promote his work as a PhD student, and to get to know him as a friend. Chris is not only a theologian, but also a missionary and pastor in Italy, where he has faithfully served with his family for many years. Chris

Foreword

brings an international and pastoral perspective on these issues from his ministry practices that prove beneficial for his charitable, balanced, yet no less straightforward perspective on Trinitarian evangelical spirituality. May this book challenge us to both think carefully and feel deeply as we labor to be good and faithful servants of our God and his Word.

Dr. Ronald T. Michener
Professor and Chair, Department of Systematic Theology
Evangelische Theologische Faculteit
Leuven, Belgium

Preface

The writing of this book started as an attempt to repackage a series of Bible messages I gave at an Italian youth camp into a sermonic booklet. However, it soon morphed into an extended theological reflection and wound up as a cathartic, ministry-centering experience for me.

The Bible studies were from a camp whose theme was "No Glory without the Cross." Its objective was to correct certain mistaken views concerning how God's people come to live in God's presence through a life lived at Calvary. On the one hand, we as camp organizers were seeking to correctively address the view held by many today that a continued presence of God in our midst is to be attained through invocation and "believing enough" irrespective of a crucified life lived daily. On the other hand, we were also eager to expose the stereotypical view of the browbeaten, oft-defeated cross-carrier as a distortion of a biblical teaching that envisions the disciple's cross as a divine instrument for getting at a life lived in God's presence through resurrection power.

As I thought more and more critically for my ever-growing booklet, I came to formulate a thesis that I wanted to test: at the root of both these unfortunate extremes lay two distinct, reductionistic views of spirituality. One so stresses the presence of God as ecstatic experiences of the Holy Spirit that it vilifies cross-centered discipleship as a wet-blanket doctrine dampening the divine fires of joy. The other places such confidence in the attainment of propositional truth as the way of knowing God that it deems the rapturous as a distraction at best, resulting in a view of the disciple's cross as a dreary classroom lesson plan. Both the form and content of the book evolved around these primary intuitions.

Preface

The present work, however, was not destined to be useful to me for intellectual discovery alone; instead, true to its roots as sermons, it was to have transformative power. By the time I finished my first major revision, I had come to realize that the process of writing the book had helped me coordinate a number of persisting personal and pastoral concerns that had plagued me over the years and caused me to waver unsatisfactorily between Word and Spirit as groundings of my own Christian spirituality. It is certainly not the case that I have exhausted the question to the degree that I will never experience conflict again. The book is not comprehensive, because it was written in order to explore rather than nail down the subject matter. For me, the ultimate contribution of writing the book was that it helped me better understand how we come to know God spiritually in the contemporary evangelical context. If it can be useful to its readers in a similar way, I will consider it a success.

Christopher Zito
Latina, Italy
January 2016

Introduction

THE SITUATION TODAY: THE "SPIRITUALIZATION" OF EVANGELICALISM

Today, especially among young people, we are witnessing what we might call the "Spiritualization" of evangelicalism.[1] As I use the term, Spiritualization is a trend in contemporary evangelical Christianity that is marked by the desire to replace a dispassionate, text-dominated faith with a more intuitive, experiential one.[2] Consequently, there is increasing pressure to conceive of the Christian faith in terms of a personal response to the divine presence—of outward and inward demonstrations understood as deriving from, pointing to, and functions of the Holy Spirit. Because of this development, evangelical churches across the globe have increasingly found themselves in the position of dealing with the internal rise of Spiritualized members, who by definition are unhappy with the traditional

---

1. Evangelicalism is notoriously difficult to demarcate. Not only does it historically take in a wide spectrum of persons, groups, denominations, and movements, but there is also no definitive consensus as to what markers actually determine what an "evangelical" is. As such, the boundaries are continuously in flux. Though there are numerous works on the subject, a *Christianity Today* review article might be a good place to start for understanding just how varied contemporary evangelicalism is. See Neff, "Top Books That Have Shaped Evangelicals," 51–55. As will become apparent throughout the course of this book, I have adapted a broad view of evangelicalism.

2. I have used the uppercase "S" for two related reasons: (a) to distance the term from the often vague, overused, and non-technical applications of "spirituality" that are currently employed in the literature, and (b) to establish it as referring to the Holy Spirit, and so specifically to Christian spirituality. For an exegetical justification of the second use, see Fee, *Listening to the Spirit*, 5. See also chapter 4 below.

emphasis—at least in practice—on "Bible over Spirit," and who tend to form what amounts to privatized interest groups within their communities.

At its worst, Spiritualization manifests itself in anti-intellectualism, hyper-pietism, sentimentalism, enthusiasm, and, at times, a kind of extraordinary or exotic mysticism. At its best, it is a sincere expression of the desire to free the church from religious rationalism, dead orthodoxy, and a concept of union with God that is more formal and abstract than personal or practical. An important, perhaps dominant strand of Western evangelicalism has historically opposed an emphasis on seeking feelings and exceptional experiences as a way of knowing God. Such evangelical Christians have traditionally perceived themselves as sober, rational, faithful followers of the Book. However, the considerable influence of the charismatic expansion over the last fifty years has drawn a caricature of this kind of believer as somehow lacking in power and worship.

For traditional evangelicals, the main objective of the disciple is to get a sound theological education, either formally or in the local church, in order to be able to rightly handle the sacred texts. This is sufficient for equipping believers for their main task in life—namely, spreading God's word and putting it into practice in the local church or mission field. With the Spiritualization of evangelicalism, however, the goal is increasingly to master how to enter into the presence of the Lord through praise, worship, and active participation in gatherings centered on liberating experiences of the Spirit. Significantly, this is often carried out with a symptomatic and sometimes systematic devaluation of the utility of doctrine for Christian spirituality.[3]

In light of this, we can affirm that the Spiritualization of evangelical churches signals a fundamental shift in the prevailing notion of what constitutes our *progressive* relatedness to God—that is, our growth in spirituality.[4] As we shall see in the first chapter, similar changes have characterized

---

3. See chapter 3 below. Some Pentecostals and charismatics would rightly contest this claim if it were made against them. See, for example, Land, *Pentecostal Spirituality*, 39. Others, at least when speaking of the post-charismatic reality, would not. See, for example, Clifton, *Pentecostal Churches in Transition*, 190. In any case, it is not my intention to associate the Spiritualization of evangelicalism strictly with the charismatic movement, though there are clear and distinct connections. I revisit this point below.

4. "Progressive" relatedness here is to be understood in contrast with "positional" and "perfected" relatedness, with the first referring to our place in Christ through justification and the latter to our union with God as it will exist in our state of glorification. As will become clearer, the aspect of spirituality on which I concentrate throughout the book is closely linked to the believer's sanctification. NB: The indiscriminate confusion

Introduction

the history of evangelicalism, broadly conceived, from its inception. In our times, a popular but helpful way of highlighting the differences is to confront models of traditional and "Spiritualized" worship approaches.

In line with the Magisterial Reformers, worship for traditional evangelicals starts with the head and only later passes through to the emotions. "Faith comes from hearing, and hearing through the word of Christ" (Rom 10:17). Christ dwells in the preaching of the word—a principle held dear by Luther and other Reformers. For this reason, reading and listening to the Bible become those human practices without which it is impossible to enjoy a proper spiritual union with God. From the ears and the eyes, the word passes through the intellect, which the Holy Spirit illumines. In line with this model of worship, the mind, assisted by the Spirit in the reading and the hearing of the Scriptures, becomes the activity center for the human being's relationship with God. Only once truth has been lifted up and confirmed can we properly engage the sentiments and evaluate experiences. According to this approach, it is crucial in worship to treat and prepare the mind with Scripture and with songs front-loaded with theological content so that the Spirit can create an environment suitable for the worship of God in Christ.

Spiritualized Christians, on the other hand, tend to emphasize a fellowship with God that takes place in the affective-experiential sphere. Instead of helping to encounter the divine presence, an active intellect can be an impediment, even when engaged in discerning biblical truths. The emphasis on repetitive and invocative music for worship indicates a strategy of spirituality based on "letting oneself go" in order to obtain visceral experiences of the Holy Spirit. It is through the heart—defined as the seat of emotions or feelings, and driven by petition, praise, and seeking—that God manifests himself to his people in worship: "But thou *art* holy, *O thou* that inhabitest the praises of Israel" (Ps 22:3).[5] Overly involving the cognitive faculties is likely to create a rational rather than spiritual environment, and consequently risks losing the opportunity to take hold of the fleeting

---

of these aspects is responsible for a great many disagreements over how Christians are to understand what spirituality is.

5. This translation from the KJV (followed by the ESV, NAU, and RSV) is contested. The NIV, siding with the Septuagint and Jerome's *Vulgate*, translates the text: "Yet you are enthroned as the Holy One; you are the praise of Israel." Clearly the meaning here is substantially different from that proposed by the KJV. For a position that supports the KJV rendering, see Craigie, *Psalms 1–50*, 194. For the contrary view, see Goldingay, *Psalms*, 327–28.

presence of the Holy Spirit, who after all behaves like the wind, blowing where and when he will.[6]

DEFINITIONS AND OBJECTIVES

While I will examine the technical aspects of Christian spirituality more thoroughly in the last chapter, it is necessary to give a working definition of the term from the start. This definition needs to be broad enough so as not to pigeonhole it before we get a chance to examine it more thoroughly, yet narrow enough to capture the essence of what I mean by it. One general designation of spirituality is "human connection with the divine."[7] Another claims that "to be spiritual means . . . that we are called to know God."[8] Combining these two descriptions, I define "spirituality" in a broad sense as *the knowledge of the divine that connects us to the divine*. Spirituality in the more narrow evangelical sense would be *the knowledge of God that unites us to God's life in accordance with the gospel*.[9]

The book in hand turns its attention to the intersection where two conceptions of spirituality collide: one grounded in *doctrine* and the other in *experience* as explanations for the primary means of progressively uniting us to God's life.[10] The main mission of this book is to clean up this chaotic crossroads within the greater evangelical metropolis, so that we might see our way clear to an evangelical spirituality that embraces the stories of both interested parties. This involves carefully sifting through the debris, throwing away the broken parts, and using the salvageable pieces from both sides.

---

6. The above phenomenology of contemporary evangelical spirituality loosely falls in line with the "vertical scale" developed by Urban T. Holmes III. See Holmes, *A History of Christian Spirituality*, 4. Holmes applied the vertical scale to the material of spirituality to draw attention to a continuum characterized on one pole by a method that emphasizes the illumination of the mind (the speculative) and on the other by a method accentuating the heart or emotions (the affective).

7. Carson, "Spirituality of the Gospel of John."

8. Holmes, *A History of Christian Spirituality*, 1.

9. For these definitions, I employ "knowledge of God" in the basic sense of "familiarity with God," irrespective of how it is obtained.

10. It is to be noted that doctrine and experience are not universally held to be valid categories of spirituality. One author, in fact, comes right out with it, writing of "the false idea that spirituality is related to *either* doctrine or experience" (Smith, *Christian Spirituality*, 8). Of course, one's view depends on how one personally defines spirituality. See below for how I employ these categories as heuristic models. See chapter 4 for how I integrate them into a biblical view of spirituality.

Introduction

In an attempt to sum up the excesses of the two sides of the debate, I take both "experience" and "doctrine" and turn them into "isms," filling them with specific content. When the suffix "-ism" is added to a word, it becomes a term that denotes a belief system. "Doctrine" is already the root of an "ism," namely "doctrinarism."[11] For this book, however, I prefer to use the term "doctrinalism" and to give it a particular content. In philosophy, the term "experientialism" commonly denotes a theory that views experience as the ultimate source of all knowledge. I maintain both the term and its general meaning, though I view it through a Christian theological lens.

By *doctrinalism*, I refer to the belief that right Christian doctrine is sufficient in and of itself as the source for knowing God in true fellowship and, consequently, for connecting us to God in order to live authentic spiritual lives. The knowledge of right doctrine does not replace faith according to this approach, though it is perceived as the necessary condition for it. The ground of true spirituality, therefore, is the faculty of illumined human reason acting upon revealed biblical teaching in bringing us deeper into a faith relationship with God. Doctrinalism does not deny the subjective aspect of spirituality, but it does reject experience as functioning positively at the ground level—that is, a personal experience of God is not a reliable or perhaps even necessary source for knowing God. Illumined intellectual knowledge of the truth is primary. This approach has been associated historically with the scholastic notion of faith as *assenso*.

On the other side of the aisle, *experientialism* asserts that we may truly know God only where unmediated experience of the Deity occurs. It is only through a direct, personal encounter with Christ that we are able to make the gospel our own in the first place. It is only as we walk in the presence of the Spirit that we work out our right standing before God in everyday life. Experientialists do not, as a matter of course, deny the importance of doctrine, though they do contend that without genuine experiences of God, the assertions of the Bible by themselves are powerless to bring us into a living relationship with God. Experientialism does not give primacy of place to a right understanding of the teachings of Scripture, as in doctrinalism, but rather to the Holy Spirit working on and in believers to create a genuine familiarity with Jesus. At a fundamental level, the intellect struggling to understand the propositions of the Bible can be a hindrance to the intuitive, even primitive, nature of true spirituality. As such, experientialism tends to view reason, the intellect, and doctrine as enemies of the work of God,

---

11. "Doctrinarism" refers to a rigid attachment to the principles of a doctrine.

wherever they clash with our ability to feel or otherwise enter into God's living presence. It is the distinctive aspect of the pietistic impulse wherever it is found and leads to the creation of emotional, subjective, and, often, charismatic Christian environments.[12]

A spirituality that is both mindful of the often-paradoxical relationship between doctrine and experience as well as reconciliatory in tone is not brand new to historical Christianity.[13] Nevertheless, it might appear suspiciously innovative to a fallen, populist, modernist mind-set unable to conceive of a reason why pluralism should not result in polarization. Indeed, precisely because we value the thrill of a good rivalry over the apparently uneventful state of reconciliation, there is often more interest in pitting doctrine against experience than in laboring to understand how they might fit together.

This book aligns itself with the latter task. It is essentially a comparative critique that concludes with a forward-looking proposal for an embodied, evangelical spirituality of the cross.[14] The reconciling effect of the cross in this proposal, however, is not only theological, but also methodological.

---

12. NB: The informed reader might be thinking at this point that doctrinalism and experientialism simply refer to the respective traditional evangelical and charismatic views of spirituality. To an extent, this is an accurate assessment, though not completely. There is admittedly an element of caricature when I associate these categories with traditional evangelicals and charismatics, respectively. This association becomes even more evident in chapters 2 and 3. However, this does not negate their usefulness. I use "doctrinalism" and "experientialism" as heuristic models that help to organize the data in two general classes so that it becomes possible to compare and contrast the varied and extensive phenomena in an orderly fashion.

13. An older attempt to reconcile doctrine and experience in a cross-shaped theology was carried out over a hundred years ago by the German pastor and theologian Christoph Blumhardt. See Zahl, *Pneumatology and Theology of the Cross*. In this critical reflection, Zahl stresses the tension in Blumhardt's theology between unmediated experience of God and classical Lutheran pneumatology that bound the action of the Spirit to the preaching of the word. According to Zahl, Blumhardt ultimately prioritized experience over a strictly empirical-inductive reading of Scripture (ibid., 57). I would not go as far as Blumhardt does in valuing experience over even a rationalist reading of the Bible, because I believe to do so sets up a false dichotomy. Nevertheless, based on the careful consideration he gave to the relationship between doctrine and experience for authentic Christian living, I consider Blumhardt a precursor to my own attempt to understand Christian spirituality in terms of doctrine and experience. This is especially true because he too couched his proposal in a theology of the cross (see below). NB: Blumhardt's works came to my attention only during the review phase of this book.

14. By "evangelical spirituality," I mean a *biblical* spirituality. See the comments by Corduan, *Mysticism*, 117.

Introduction

That is to say, it not only speaks of how fractured humanity is reconciled to itself in Christ, both individually and corporately, but also to how doctrine and experience are brought together in order to ensure Christians might walk in a fully-orbed spirituality. In the service of linking what it means to be spiritual to what it means to be a New Covenant, dying-to-self disciple of Jesus Christ, the proposal seeks to bring together two aspects of Christian spirituality that are commonly perceived of as diametrically opposed.

Ultimately, therefore, I am interested in the polarizing effect that siding with doctrine on the one hand or experience on the other has on how evangelicals both perceive and live out their spirituality. The didactic goal of this book is to provide our churches with a critical reflection on these two conflicting but influential views of spirituality so that the current generation of evangelicals might engage in healthy self-criticism, reviewing and, perhaps, reforming its ideas of what it means to be spiritual Christians.

METHOD

To accomplish these goals, I work in a critical-reflective-phenomenological way. By combining historical research, critical reflection, and observation of the contemporary phenomena, I attempt first to expose the fundamental errors of both doctrinalism and experientialism by testing their theological, biblical, and philosophical presuppositions and methodology. Secondly, and in light of this critique, I reevaluate the claims of each group as to what is constitutive of true Christian spirituality. What I do not do is provide a comprehensive examination of evangelical spirituality. There simply is not enough space, nor is it my intention to provide such an analysis. The reader, therefore, will not come away with an extensive knowledge of all the issues. Rather, I have concentrated on two polarized positions concerning the roles of doctrine and experience for knowing God. By working in this way, I am able to show how both approaches lead to an unbalanced, erroneous, and even idolatrous view of Christian spirituality.[15]

In our contemporary setting, it is hardly necessary to justify my choices for the "partners" in the present dialogue. The importance of the debate between doctrine and experience in today's evangelical setting is as axiomatic as a historical phenomenon can be. Whoever is even modestly familiar with the broader evangelical world has certainly encountered a number of the

---

15. This idolatry manifests itself in proportion to the extremes to which one goes in pursuing doctrinalist or experientialist beliefs and practices.

arguments presented in this book. In common parlance, this confrontation is sometimes characterized in terms of an opposition of head and heart and sometimes of word and Spirit. In the academic world, specialists sometimes describe the problem in terms of conflicts between objectivity and subjectivity, rationalism and existentialism, or Scholasticism and Pietism.

Even though the debate is self-evident simply by observing the life of the contemporary evangelical scene, I have further justified both the authenticity and timeliness of my thesis in the first chapter of this book by showing that the topic under discussion has a long and sometimes infamous history in the church. Starting with the Reformation, I trace the controversy between doctrine and experience in Protestantism up to the present divergence between traditional evangelicalism and the Pentecostal-charismatic strain. Some might be tempted to skip this part and, to a certain extent, could without losing the thread of the overall argument. However, I would encourage readers to explore the history of the debate, because it opens our eyes to the reality that we do not practice faith in a vacuum but rather in a lively and dynamic conversation, which arguably has its origin in the very writings of the New Testament itself.

In the two successive chapters, I resume the discussion on which the previous historical survey ended, dealing respectively with doctrinalism and experientialism as they manifest themselves in broader contemporary evangelicalism. In these sections, I critically reflect on the claims of both groups as to what constitutes the knowledge of God that unites us to God in genuine, gospel-centered fellowship. Despite my sometimes severe criticisms of both camps, I hope to be fair in my treatments and approach both with the compassion and love that should characterize all our judgments as Christians.

In the fourth chapter, I briefly survey the history of spirituality in the church and in contemporary culture before circling back and ending with a critical reflection on what the Bible and specifically the New Testament has to say to the various historical and current conceptions of the subject. The result is the recognition of a common deficiency in both approaches—namely, that both doctrinalism and experientialism provide us with derivative Neoplatonic spiritualities in which the practical lordship of the Holy Spirit has limited application or, at any rate, an artificially imposed, ultimately powerless function for helping us live our union with God. These conclusions point to the necessity, as I argue, for a Spirit-led, embodied spirituality of the cross going forward into the middle of the twenty-first century.

Chapter 1

Doctrinalism and Experientialism in the Evangelical Tradition

> What has been is what will be, and what has been done is what will be done, and there is nothing new under the sun.[1]

As I have already suggested, the contemporary church is at a crossroads with respect to the debate over whether Christian spirituality is more a matter of doctrine or experience, head or heart, word or Spirit. How did we arrive at this crossroads? As the Preacher said centuries ago, there is nothing new under the sun. Our present is wrapped up in our past; in unknown but concrete ways, our past was determining its future.

Throughout church history, conflicts of belief have often turned into reasons for hostility and polarization. What could have been opportunities to expand and enrich the knowledge of the truth through peaceful conversation have instead caused incalculable damage to the name of Christ. Notwithstanding this unfortunate trajectory, the polemical nature of the church has not usually prevented the deepening of our understanding, but only reshaped and, perhaps, prolonged it. The purpose of the present chapter is to provide a historical grounding and framework for the critical

---

1. Eccl 1:9. NB: All biblical citations, unless otherwise noted, are taken from the English Standard Version (ESV).

reflections on doctrinalism and experientialism that are to follow in the second and third chapters.

In the short space I have, it is not possible to trace all the historical, social, philosophical, theological, psychological, and spiritual twists and turns of the church's journey from Pentecost to the present. Therefore, I will be guided in this brief historical account by a very specific thread: the theological and practical back-and-forth emphasis between doctrine and experience in Western Protestantism from the Reformation to the present. Historically speaking, these phenomena are best represented in terms of the enduring conflict between scholastic and pietist leanings throughout Protestant church history. For this reason, I have favored these terms throughout the chapter, though the notions of doctrinalism and experientialism are never far from mind.

SCHOLASTICISM, PURITANISM, AND PIETISM

Modern traditional evangelicalism has its roots in the various incarnations of so-called Protestant scholasticism, the latter of which reared its head for the first time not very long after Luther's Reformation, maturing in the seventeenth century. While Luther placed emphasis on the action of faith as trust and on the object of faith as the gospel, the Protestant scholastics after him adopted the prevailing medieval view of faith as mental assent to certain truths about God.[2] As a result, there was a great effort on the part of the Protestant scholastics to order all Christian truths handed down to them by the Reformers into a single, defensible system. The objective of this mammoth task was apologetic—that is, to establish the newly founded Reformed faith on the firmest rational foundations possible.

With this undertaking, the Scholastics adopted a methodology that embraced philosophy and logic as a means of assisting the building of coherent systems of Protestant doctrine.[3] The Scholastic Calvinists in par-

---

2. González, *Essential Theological Terms*, s.v. "Faith," 61. González maintains that medieval scholasticism spoke of faith both as the act of believing (*fides qua creditur*) and as the content of faith (*fides quae creditur*). According to the former, the most important thing is trust, while for the latter it is assent to what is to be believed. González also confirms that faith as assent goes back to patristic theology, but not only in the sense of a mental agreement—the human will also held an important role. In addition, faith was not seen as complete without hope and love.

3. Olson, *Story of Christian Theology*, 455. Contemporary scholars such as Richard A. Mueller, David Steinmetz, and H. A. Oberman have revolutionized studies on Protestant

ticular turned to the Aristotelian method for help in this task. The result was the elevation of theological method and of human reason in general to prominent positions in the investigation and defense of the faith.[4]

Within Calvinistic circles, however, a movement arose that offset the methodological emphasis of the Scholastics. The Puritans of Great Britain did not downplay the importance of doctrine but instead placed an emphasis on religious practice and devotion that was at odds with the objectives of the Scholastics.[5] In this way, they achieved a balance that has rarely been seen in the history of the church, providing an expression of the Christian faith in which the life of the intellect and that of felt devotion were not viewed as diametrically opposed but rather as two sides of the same operation.

It may be argued from a certain perspective that from the Reformation until today the distinctive feature of the history of Protestantism has been a continuous back-and-forth between the rationalist tendency on the one side and the experientialist or affective one on the other. Just one hundred years after the birth of Puritanism in England, in fact, Deism emerged as a powerful force in the same country to combat the Puritan "intransigence." Unlike the earlier Scholastics, the Deists embraced rationalism as a substitute for faith based on revelation. By identifying itself completely with the rational project of the Enlightenment, Deism soon became an ethical and anti-dogmatic religious philosophy. Its distinctive theological contribution (especially the "Cambridge Platonists") was the proposal of a transcendent God who started the creation only to abandon it to the dominion of natural laws that, consequently, were discoverable by reason.

This philosophy was important in the formation of the ideology of both the French and American Revolutions, but its spread to Germany helped incite one of the most anti-rationalist Christian movements ever seen in the history of the church. Pietism blossomed from within German

---

Scholasticism, leading to much more positive conclusions concerning the theological continuity between the original Reformers and their Scholastic successors. Reflecting on these studies, Willem Van Asselt indicates that based on historical, philosophical, and theological grounds, a clear distinction must be made between the rationalism of the Enlightenment and the use of rational argumentation by the Scholastics in matters of faith. Specifically, post-Reformation scholastics did not show any signs in their writings that they believed reason and revelation to be equal or that they were two distinct sources of knowledge (Van Asselt, "Protestant Scholasticism," 272).

4. McGrath, *Historical Theology*, 169.
5. Breward, "Puritan Theology," 550.

Lutheranism and was hostile not only to the rationalism of the Deists, but also to the emphasis the Scholastics had given to doctrine. The criticism of the Pietists was that Scholasticism obscured the need for a "living faith" among believers.[6] At the heart of the Pietist project, therefore, was the search, shared with the Puritans, for a personal experience of God that would allow the believer to live a truly sanctified life.[7]

Unhappy with how the Scholastics had mutated trust (*fiducia*) in God into a mental assent (*assenso*) to a body of doctrines methodically defined by the Lutheran theologians, the Pietists claimed that the theological insights of Luther were not to be classified in minute detail in the interests of systematization. Rather, the theology of the great Reformer was intended to produce a reformation in the life of the believer. This transformation would be manifested primarily in a deeply personal relationship with God and would be expressed in a lifestyle that reflected God's will. It was the latter view, in fact, that became the hallmark of the movement.[8]

REVIVALISM AND PRINCETON THEOLOGY

Deism and Pietism in the late seventeenth and eighteenth centuries constituted two divergent religious reactions to Protestant scholasticism: full-blown rationalism and religious personalism. It was in the fourth decade of the eighteenth century that Puritanism and Pietism "cross-pollinated" to give birth to modern evangelicalism in the revivalism of Great Britain and North America.[9] Despite being a movement of the heart and emotions, the First Great Awakening (1735–1744) was not characterized by the kind of mystic Pietism found, for example, in the Quakers (1647). Both the American Jonathan Edwards (Calvinist, Yale) that the Englishman John Wesley (Arminian, Oxford) were important theologians, well versed in both Christian Scripture and philosophy (Edwards was, in fact, a philosopher). Yet both men rejected rationalism and the scholastic method in order to pursue a practical and biblical revivalism that emerged out of a love for the Scriptures, a great respect for the theology of the Puritans, and Pietism's search for an intensely personal relationship with God.[10]

---

6. McGrath, *Historical Theology*, 169.
7. Grenz, *Renewing the Center*, 40.
8. Ibid., 41–42.
9. Ibid., 44.
10. See the chart in Cairns, *Christianity through the Centuries*, 376. For a classic

Doctrinalism and Experientialism in the Evangelical Tradition

Whatever partnership may have existed between the Calvinist and Arminian branches during the first Great Awakening began unraveling within gospel-centered Christianity during the Second Great Awakening in America (1800–1835). While the Arminian Wesley and the Calvinist Whitefield cooperated with each other in ministry, remaining friends despite the rocky times their relationship sometimes endured, the antagonism of the American revivalist Charles Finney towards the Calvinism of his Presbyterian background was fierce. His very emotional approach to revivalism created some formidable enemies for him, particularly at the new seminary in Princeton, which had been founded in 1812 by the General Assembly of the Presbyterian Church. Indeed, from this time onward within evangelicalism as it is broadly conceived, there can be seen among the offspring of Princeton on the one hand and Finney's brand of revivalism on the other a clear demarcation between neo-Scholastic and neo-Pietist strands—or, to insert the terms used in this book, between doctrinalist and experientialists approaches to the Christian faith.

Though Deism proper was on the decline, its influence spread throughout the West on the coattails of enlightened modernity. What resulted was a succession of Christian rationalist sects such as Unitarianism (1825), Mormonism (1827), Seventh-day Adventists (1846), and, a little later, Jehovah's Witnesses (1872) and Christian Science (1879).

By maintaining a strict Reformed orthodoxy, Princeton theology avoided the rationalism that plagued the emerging sects; nevertheless, it yielded to the modern spirit in a different way. Indeed, the modernity of Princeton was not characterized by the liberal notion that reason is the final arbiter of all matters relating to the truth. For these faithful men, only the Scriptures assisted by the illumination of the Holy Spirit had this role. What distinguished Princeton theology from earlier evangelicals, rather, was the strong confidence placed in the *scientific method* as a means of uncovering divinely revealed truth in the Scriptures. In developing the empirical method for the study of the Bible, theologians such as Archibald Alexander, Charles Hodge, A. A. Hodge, and Benjamin Warfield were responsible for what many have considered the rise of a proper evangelical scholasticism.

The driving force of this new scholasticism was clearly an apologetic impulse to defend Reformed orthodoxy from three imminent threats: (a) the rationalism of Deism and Unitarianism; (b) the emotional revivalism

---

Calvinist portrayal of the union of the intellect, the will, and the emotions in Christian conversion, see Jonathan Edwards' *The Religious Affections* (1746).

of Finney; and (c) the subjectivity of German liberalism.[11] Arguably, the most important innovation in this respect was the re-conceptualization of the nature of the Bible. Warfield and others shifted away from the concept of the Scriptures as primarily a living channel through which God spoke, adopting a notion of the Bible as a storehouse of empirical data clearly observable to human reason. In his *Systematic Theology* of 1871, Charles Hodge clearly suggests such a view, as can be surmised by the following tract:

> [T]he duty of the Christian theologian is to ascertain, collect, and combine all the facts which God has revealed concerning himself and our relation to Him. These facts are all in the Bible. This is true, because everything revealed in nature, and in the constitution of man concerning God and our relation to Him, is contained and authenticated in Scripture. It is in this sense that "the Bible, and the Bible alone, is the religion of Protestants."[12]

Because of this mind-set, Princeton came to understand the task of systematic theology as the "coordinating and harmonizing of the axioms of Scripture, which are self-evident as well as clear and distinct," and thus open to scientific investigation.[13] Such Christian empiricism falls in line with scholastic rationalism, insofar as it understands the written revelation as "the disclosure of a higher truth that nonetheless stands in continuity with rational or natural truth."[14]

This approach to the Bible and theology tended to replace faith with human intellectual capacity *as the starting point* for understanding

---

11. Sundberg, "Princeton School."

12. Hodge, *Systematic Theology*, 1:11. Despite such a clear dependence on empirical method for biblical interpretation, Mark Noll has argued that Charles Hodge "gives much more scope in the theological enterprise to the 'moral nature,' the messages of the 'heart,' and the work of the Holy Spirit" than his contemporaries at Princeton (Noll, *Princeton Theology*, 117). Indeed, he held a view of the Bible as self-authenticating, arguing that its truth need not be demonstrated by proof. In this way, Noll asserts that Hodge avoided giving primacy to the rationalist Scottish Common Sense Realism adopted by Princeton theology as well as the evidentialist apologetics of his predecessor Archibald Alexander and successor B. B. Warfield (ibid.). These and other considerations have not always been honestly and thoroughly engaged in contemporary critiques of Princeton theology, though not even sympathizers of the movement claim that it totally escaped the "rationalist" and "scholastic" labels. See, for example, Battle, "Charles Hodge"; McConnel, "Old Princeton Apologetics."

13. See Bloesch, *Life, Ministry, and Hope*, 268.

14. Ibid., 270.

revelation. In this way, Princeton methodology effectively reversed Anselm's hermeneutical dictum *fides quaerens intellectum* ("faith seeking understanding").[15] For Princeton theology, therefore, it was no longer a question of faith grounding and guiding the search for understanding, but rather of natural reason employed in the services of the empirical method applied to the Bible, which made faith in revelation a possibility in the first place.

According to this method, mental assent to the claims of the Bible functions as faith. This created a sharp tension within Princeton's Calvinistic theology. For on the one hand, there is no faith without the Holy Spirit giving it to the elected believer. On the other hand, there is a sense in which the Holy Spirit was not the executive means of faith but rather a kind of assistant to human reason. Despite its insistence that divine revelation was the source of all true knowledge of the gospel and that this truth could be supernaturally illumined only by the work of the Holy Spirit, Princeton theology was rationalist because it promoted the idea that, in the final analysis, it is the human intellect scientifically applied to evangelical truth that ultimately grounds personal faith.

The magnitude of this paradigm shift within orthodox Christianity was not lost on Princeton's contemporary Reformed colleagues in other parts of the world. For example, Abraham Kuyper of the Amsterdam school argued that the empiricist, common-sense presuppositions of the Princeton theologians were not self-evident to human reason but were instead Scripture-given and to be embraced by faith. It is impossible, therefore, to establish them on the grounds of human reason, as Princeton attempted to do in accordance with its apologetic agenda for doing theology.[16] Kuyper, in fact, accused the Princeton theologians of wanting to establish a rational apologetic as the basis for doing theology. The Princeton school returned the favor by calling the Amsterdam school fideists.[17]

On the grassroots side of revivalism, there were important figures and new movements that centered on the more practical aspects of Christian life, like mission, evangelism, the work of the Holy Spirit in sanctification, and an ecclesiology that became more and more open to the laity. England saw the beginning of modern missions led by William Carey (1793), the emergence of the Plymouth Brethren with the likes of John Darby and

---

15. Ironically, Anselm is often referred to (mistakenly?) as the father of Scholasticism.
16. Klooster, "How Reformed Theologians 'Do Theology,'" 233–34.
17. Hesselink, "Some Distinctive Contributions," 430.

George Müeller (1820), and later the pioneering social-evangelistic work of William Booth and his Salvation Army (1878).

THE HOLINESS MOVEMENT, LIBERALISM, AND FUNDAMENTALISM

One of the most important pietist influences at the turn of the twentieth century was the Holiness movement, which arose from the revivalism of Wesley and Finney. The linchpin of this North American movement was, as the name suggests, holiness and particularly the belief that there is a separate and secondary work or experience of the Holy Spirit after justification. From this movement comes the search for a "higher life" with respect to "conventional" Christianity as well as a reinterpretation of the concept of holiness in the Methodist experience of Christian perfection, by which sin can be eradicated from the heart of the believer. The main event on the road to perfection was often understood in terms of a "baptism of the Holy Spirit," from Methodist origin, indicating the starting point for a renewed life of witness and service to the gospel.

Out of the Holiness movement arose the British counterpart: the Higher Life or Keswick movement founded in 1875. More than an organized movement, it consisted of a series of lectures, conferences, and literature promoted by a variety of members from different denominations and confessions.[18] In many ways, Keswick brought a balance to the Holiness movement, as it proposed a "middle way" to the different theological currents of the American movement by speaking in uniform terms of a "suppression" of sinful nature. Furthermore, some adherents remained open to different interpretations of the baptism of the Holy Spirit, while some rejected outright any such experience as explanatory for the higher life. Keswick also provided the Holiness movement with a certain level of prestige due to the fame, character, ministries, and influences of many of its participants, including E. M. Bounds, Andrew Murray, F. B. Meyers, Oswald Chambers, D. L. Moody, R. A. Torrey, and A. B. Simpson.

At the beginning of the twentieth century, Princeton theology became the basis on which American fundamentalism stood up to challenge the Protestant liberalism that had significantly infiltrated traditional denominations. Liberalism in Europe was rooted in the German Enlightenment

---

18. Indeed, it was known as the Keswick movement because it was promoted at conventions held at the English market town of Keswick.

of the nineteenth century. Brought to the fore by Friedrich Schleiermacher (d. 1834), liberalism was a strange mixture of enlightenment rationalism and German Pietism. Perhaps it would not be an overstatement to say that Schleiermacher's liberalism was the humanistic reception of the pietistic impulse, insofar as it adopted Pietism's emphasis on the experiential aspect of our relationship with God.[19] What was novel in liberal theology was the elevation of a singular experience—namely, the universal religious sentiment of *dependence on God*. For early liberalism, the felt need of God universally experienced by all people replaced the revealed word as the source of faith and became the object to which theology was to turn its attention.[20]

It was this revolutionary turn toward subjectivism from the liberals that motivated Charles Hodge of Princeton to conceive of conservative theology as primarily an *apologetic* task to be accomplished by the use of rigorous scientific method on the Bible. Hodge's approach reflected the mind-set that Christianity was something essentially reactionary and defensive. Indeed, the apologetic theology practiced by Hodge did not reach back to orthodox statements of the faith in order to enrich the evolving contemporary discussion but did so to instead fossilize traditional expressions of doctrine over and against the progressive liberal threat. As an archeologist might photograph a fresh dig site in order to "freeze" the ancient city as it had been preserved, Hodge's objective was to capture a certain expression of Christian truth in order to point to it as objective and final. Rather than encouraging the building of bridges from the church to the modern world through creative contemporary application of biblical and historical orthodoxy, the Princeton approach sought to build a wall around the church to protect it from its various enemies. In this way, Princeton provided a defensive methodology with which conservative Christian orthodoxy could defend itself against liberalism's emergent subjectivity. While believing in the personal and experiential dimensions of faith, Hodge promoted a view of Christianity that was ultimately reducible to a system of doctrines to be properly expounded and believed. Consequently, whoever believed in doctrines thus formulated was a true Christian. To reject or even doubt any one

---

19. Cf. Barth, *Protestant Theology*, 84–144. In this book, Barth claimed that Pietism arose as a result of a disproportionate elevation of man and so was the precursor of liberalism. However, it is generally accepted that most Pietists viewed themselves as miserable sinners saved by a personal experience of God's grace. After the experience of grace, however, the believer was indeed elevated. See Nichols, "Search for a Pentecostal Structure," 58.

20. Franco, *Lexicon: Dizionario Dei Teologi*, s.v. "Schleiermacher Friedrich," 1121–24.

part of the system was tantamount to rejecting the whole of the objectively verifiable truth and was therefore either error or heresy.[21]

"Inspired by the great revivals of the evangelist Dwight Layman Moody . . . dismayed and appalled by the growing influence of liberal theology, and energized by the resurgent Protestant orthodoxy of Warfield and others,"[22] Fundamentalism was a calculated response to the threats made by liberalism and the Social Gospel to basic conservative doctrines and beliefs. These beliefs included the inspiration of Scripture, the deity of Christ, the Trinity, the virgin birth, the fall, the penal substitution of Christ, and the bodily resurrection, ascension, and return of Christ, and so on.

Fundamentalism began in the 1870s as a series of decisions made within the historic churches to separate themselves from denominations and universities that had accepted the liberal project. In the first decades, it was a vital and unified movement whose primary objective was to defend and propagate the supernatural gospel of the historic faith. A major strength was its ability to sustain alliances between pietists and dispensationalists, Calvinists and Arminians, and Episcopal and independent churches.[23] It was during this period that modern "evangelical conservatism" started taking shape. However, being the fruit of revival on the one hand and Princeton theology on the other, it was only a matter of time before the movement began to fracture and divide.

The more pietistic side of fundamentalism was strongly influenced by the dispensationalism and premillennialism of John Darby from the Plymouth brethren, and later by C. I. Scofield, especially through the Scofield Reference Bible (1909).[24] In the period from 1876 to 1895, Darby organized a series of interdenominational meetings that revealed the importance of the rigorous study of the Scriptures and promoted his emerging dispensationalist eschatology. It was during these meetings that the outline for what would become fundamentalism was established. The movement proper, however, would only emerge later, on the shoulders of the various confessional statements and especially the twelve-volume document *The*

21. See Olson, *Story of Christian Theology*, 559.
22. Ibid., 561.
23. Conn, *Contemporary World Theology*, 119.
24. Chan and Ward, "Pietism," 655. In this article, the authors write of the critical role Pietist theology and spirituality played in the formation of various evangelical movements such as the Moravian Brethren, Methodism, the Plymouth Brethren, and the Holiness and Pentecostal movements. Members from most of these groups took active parts in the original fundamentalist movement.

Fundamentals, which was published between 1909 and 1912 by authors from a variety of Protestant denominations.[25] For a time, this monumental undertaking was able to unite in a common mission such diverse ecclesial and academic figures as H. G. Moule, R. A. Torrey, A. T. Pierson, and C. T. Studd, who were associated with the Keswick movement; dispensationalists such as C. I. Scofield, Arno C. Gaebalein, and W. H. Griffith Thomas; and more scholastically-inclined theologians such as B. B Warfield, the Scottish Presbyterian James Orr, and J. Gresham Machen, who eventually left Princeton when it became too liberal in order to begin the conservative Westminster Theological Seminary in Pennsylvania.

Fundamentalism reached its zenith in the 1920s in the United States, when the so-called "modernist/fundamentalist controversy" came to a head in 1925. In the famous Scopes Monkey Trial of that same year, the movement fell out of favor with the public through the biased efforts of the media, which ceaselessly caricaturized the fundamentalists as medieval obscurantists.[26] After this public humiliation, the branch of fundamentalism derived from revivalism began to retreat to an increasingly defensive and isolationist position. In the years immediately following World War II, the reactionary tendency that had always characterized fundamentalism in general began to prevail over this subgroup in particular. Thus so-called neo-fundamentalism was born, characterized by an extreme dispensationalism, an excessive emotionalism, an aversion to theology, the negligence of ethical issues, pietistic individualism, a "default" fear of cultural challenges to the gospel, and the tendency to withdraw from society.[27]

The most important element affecting the unity of conservative Christianity was neo-fundamentalism's increasing entrenchment in dispensationalist and premillennialist positions. The rift grew to such proportions that in some cases non-dispensationalists were labeled as incipient liberals. This lead the Reformed branch of the movement to became increasingly reluctant to be associated with the "fundamentalist" label to the point of permanently disassociating itself from the term.[28] The acrimonious division was only the first step in a series of successive subdivisions of funda-

---

25. Menzies, "Reformed Roots of Pentecostalism," 266–67.

26. In this trial, a teacher from a school in Tennessee was charged and tried for violation of the "Tennessee's Butler Act," which prohibited teaching the theory of evolution in the schools of Tennessee.

27. See Conn, *Contemporary World Theology*, 121.

28. Ibid., 119–21.

mentalism that saw the original mission deteriorate from "a biblical call for separation from unbelief to an unbiblical reactionary spirit."[29] It was during these years that modern-day evangelicalism blossomed as a countermovement, with the stated aim of bringing evangelical theology back into the conversation with the wider (Christian) world.

NEO-ORTHODOXY AND PENTECOSTALISM

In the midst of the struggle between fundamentalists and liberal factions, two movements emerged that would mark the conscience of evangelicalism for years to come: neo-orthodoxy and Pentecostalism. At first glance, the two movements could not be more dissimilar. However, knowing the historical trajectories of these two movements is essential if we are to put the contemporary doctrinalist/experientialist question within evangelicalism into perspective.

In the history of the twentieth-century church, it was not only the fundamentalists who protested against the liberals. Already in 1915, Karl Barth, recently graduated and in a new pastorate in Switzerland, was dismayed by of the lack of suitable material for preaching to be found within his liberal theology professors' body of writings. By that time, the liberals had already moved beyond the pietism of Schleiermacher to their own brand of literary scholasticism, which was called biblical criticism. In response to the dearth of pastoral materials produced by this method, Barth began to rediscover the Bible as a source of life for his flock rather than as material useful solely for academic study. This led him to write a commentary on the Epistle to the Romans, which at the time was famously described as a bombshell dropped on the playground of theologians.

It had such an explosive effect because in opposition to the trend of modernist critical method, Barth refused to make use of contemporary hermeneutics as an excuse to detach the language of the Bible from its content. In other words, he re-introduced the idea of the "word of God" into the wider theological discussion of the universities. The critical method was used as a preparation for understanding the Scriptures, but it was unable in and of itself to achieve the interpretation of the text. Barth was convinced that the interpreter had to let the content speak for itself, without the scholastic dissections of the critics. This did not mean, however, that critical study was to be rejected in favor of a strictly pastoral or practical

---

29. Ibid., 121.

Doctrinalism and Experientialism in the Evangelical Tradition

exegesis. Nevertheless, for Barth, to be truly critical one had to allow the Bible to speak in its own voice.[30]

In a fundamental way, Barth's approach to Scripture was the antithesis of the scholastic method. As discussed above, scholasticism of any age seeks to establish Christian truths on the firmest possible rational foundations. Therefore, it is fair to consider it an *apologetic* approach to the faith aimed at demonstrating through rational proof that Christianity is absolutely or, in any case, eminently reasonable. When scholasticism is applied to the doctrines of the Bible, as it was in both critical liberalism and Princeton fundamentalism, the result are books such as *The Battle for the Bible*,[31] in which the truth of the message of Christianity is subjected to the sometimes overbearing defense of a particular doctrine of language and interpretation, such as can be found in most fundamentalist defenses of the doctrine of biblical infallibility.[32]

The neo-orthodoxy of Barth, Emil Brunner, and the Niebuhr brothers was a reaction against the idealism and rationalism of modern theology; at the same time, it was a search for a more holistic view of the faith. Significantly, both liberals and fundamentalists attacked neo-orthodoxy for the same reason—a supposed lack of "rationality" at the level of its theological presuppositions. Since neo-orthodoxy emphasized the transcendence of God and humans' inability to know God apart from an existential encounter with the Scriptures, liberals perceived it as an irrational escape into supernaturalism and obscurantism—or, as some snidely called it, "fundamentalism with good manners."[33] On the other hand, fundamentalists, who firmly believed in the supernaturalism of the Bible, were suspicious of the emphasis the neo-orthodox placed on God's transcendence at the expense of the historical aspects of the gospel. Because people like Barth and Brunner rejected the Princeton doctrine of the Bible and its literalist hermeneutic, both fundamentalists and the then-emerging neo-evangelicals were suspicious and often hostile towards them.[34]

---

30. Treier, *Introducing Theological Interpretation of Scripture*, 16–18.
31. Lindsell, *Battle for the Bible*.
32. See Raschke, *Next Reformation*, 124.
33. See Olson, *Story of Christian Theology*, 571.
34. See the comprehensive critique of Barth by the Princeton and then Westminster theologian Cornelius Van Til, e.g., Van Til, *New Modernism*; ibid., *Christianity and Barthianism*.

DOCTRINE AND EXPERIENCE

Liberals and evangelicals also found themselves unlikely bedfellows with respect to the neo-orthodox approach to the word of God. The neo-orthodox argued that it was neither written revelation nor human reason that made the Scriptures real, but rather the encounter one had with Christ, who is the living word, *through* the reading of the Bible. Whatever else one could say about neo-orthodoxy, its doctrine of the word of God created a theological environment in which a pietist doctrine of the Scriptures could get a serious hearing in the academy for perhaps the first time since the origin of Pietism in the seventeenth century.[35]

Another influential movement that arose at the turn of the twentieth century was Pentecostalism. Pentecostals did not involve themselves directly in the fundamentalist controversy against the liberals, although it is clear that they fully aligned themselves with the doctrinal values fundamentalism advocated. They were also marked by the characteristics attributed above to the revivalist branch of fundamentalism, especially to the Holiness movement out of which it grew. Once it became clear that the Reformed (i.e., Princeton-influenced) fundamentalists were aggressively opposed to the Pentecostal teachings on the baptism of the Holy Spirit and tongues-speaking, Pentecostals resigned themselves to this rejection without losing their enthusiasm.[36] The fundamentalists' rejection of these Pentecostal allies against liberalism speaks volumes to the true depths of the divide between the scholastic and pietist strains of Christianity in general and the theology of Princeton and Pentecostal distinctives in particular.

The Princeton scholar B. B. Warfield erected an insurmountable barrier between the two groups when he declared that the spiritual gifts most valued by the Pentecostals actually ceased at the end of the apostolic age. With the advent of the New Testament as the standard for faith for the

---

35. Ironically, neo-orthodoxy was bitterly anti-Pietist. In particular, Barth criticized the popular piety of his time. However, there is also a sense in which neo-orthodoxy laid the theological groundwork on which neo-pietism could stand in the contemporary academic discussion. Indeed, the Lutheran Carl E. Braaten speaks favorably of a "neo-orthodox pietism"—that is, one that upholds "pure doctrine" but does not lose itself in a battle for the infallibility of the Bible (Braaten, *Because of Christ*, 3).

36. Menzies, "Non-Wesleyan Pentecostalism," 200. In the beginning at least, the antagonism seemed unilateral. Menzies singles out the meeting of the World Christian Fundamental Association in 1928 in which a resolution was adopted that denied any connection with or endorsement of the "tongues movement" (ibid., 210). Menzies also documents the exhortation of *Pentecostal Evangel* magazine to respond to this decision with love and confidence that one day there could be a real communion between the two movements.

church, Warfield argued that there was no more need for the authoritative divine gifts such as apostleship, prophecy, and tongues. It is clear that on this point, classical Pentecostalism, with its emphasis on the gift of tongues as evidence of the baptism of the Holy Spirit, would have to distance itself not only from Princeton theology, but also from fundamentalism as a whole, which almost universally accepted Warfield's doctrine.[37]

No less divisive was how Pentecostals perceived themselves within the arc of church history. According to the Catholic charismatic Peter Hocken, the early Pentecostals saw themselves in terms of performance and uniqueness. From the start, the "Pentecostal" phenomenon was perceived by its members as the culmination of the earlier revivalist movements of the Spirit starting with Wesley, passing through Finney, and continuing on through the Holiness movement.[38]

As the culmination of all the previous movements and the result of decades of prayer by believers, Pentecostalism also perceived itself as unique in the history of the post-apostolic church. Rooted in the Azusa Street Revival of 1906 and justified on the basis of Jas 5: 7, Joel 2:23, and Job 37:6, Pentecostals believed themselves to have experienced the "latter rain," repossessing for our day the blessing of Pentecost—the baptism of the Holy Spirit with its concomitant gift of speaking in tongues. Through Pentecostalism, therefore, God went beyond what he had previously done in the Holiness and revivalist movements. The very fact that they called themselves "Pentecostals" and described the movement of the Spirit as the "latter rain" is evidence enough that they understood themselves in a unique light. In addition to this, the message they preached was known among themselves as the "Full Gospel."[39]

Clearly, the Pentecostal call for a return to the "Full Gospel" with all its gifts of the Spirit was incompatible with the cessationism of Warfield and Reformed fundamentalist theologians. As suggested above, however, it was not totally at variance with the fundamentalist branch arising from the revivalist tradition. The Pentecostal interest in healing and other signs of the presence of the Holy Spirit, for example, had precedents within

---

37. Dayton, "Theological Roots of Pentecostalism," 5.

38. Hocken, "Pentecostal-Charismatic Movement," 32. This continuity with the revivalist movement is marked by Pentecostalism's adoption and incorporation of revivalist terms such as "revival," "awakening," and "outpouring" to describe the work God was accomplishing in and through them.

39. Ibid., 33–34.

Methodism's pietist influences. The doctrine of the baptism of the Holy Spirit, on the other hand, had an immediate antecedent in the Holiness movement.[40]

Notwithstanding the influence of the Holiness movement in the formation of Pentecostalism, the former did not embrace the hallmarks of the latter. Some, like A. B. Simpson, were neutral or vague, while others were blatantly hostile to the claims of the Pentecostals, particularly to the need to speak in tongues as a sign of the baptism of the Spirit. Thus, even someone like the revivalist Evan Roberts, who witnessed many bizarre behaviors during the Great Awakening of Wales (1904–1905), would seven years later co-author the classic book *War on the Saints* together with the explicit anti-Pentecostal Jessie Penn-Lewis. Moreover, Penn-Lewis was active in both Keswick and the publication of *The Fundamentals* and had herself been influenced by Andrew Murray, who is generally recognized as one of the most important influences on Pentecostalism. Evans and Penn-Lewis were not the only examples of prominent Keswick people that distanced themselves from Pentecostalism. R. A. Torrey, the president of Moody Bible Institute in Chicago and a strong progenitor of a doctrine of the baptism of the Holy Spirit, allegedly said that the Pentecostal movement was in no way of God, founded as it was by a sodomite.[41]

This tension between Keswick and the Pentecostals lends credence to the argument that Pentecostalism was not a simple sub-section of fundamentalist evangelicalism but was rather "a major new block in Christianity."[42] If the experientialism associated with the Holiness movement was a counterbalance to the scholasticism of Princeton theology and Reformed fundamentalism, Pentecostalism was a veritable protest of the all-encompassing role of doctrine for the faith. With its emphasis on the baptism of the Holy Spirit and tongues-speaking, Pentecostals raised immediate religious experience to a supreme place in the order of things.

---

40. Ibid., 34n3. Of particular interest in this regard was the influence of the Canadian A. B. Simpson on Pentecostalism. From 1887 onwards, Simpson, founder of the Christian and Missionary Alliance and participant in the Keswick movement, taught that the four roles of Jesus was as Savior, Sanctifier, Healer, and Coming Lord. Essentially, the Pentecostals adopted Simpson's model for their "Fourfold Gospel," changing "Sanctifier" into "Baptizer with the Holy Spirit."

41. Cited in Synan, *Holiness-Pentecostal Tradition*, 146.

42. Hocken, "Pentecostal-Charismatic Movement," 45.

Doctrinalism and Experientialism in the Evangelical Tradition

(NEO-)EVANGELICALISM

According to the historian Derek Tidball, one of the most important occurrences on the theological scene after World War II was the growth of evangelical scholarship and its relationship to the academy.[43] It was an important phenomenon because by that time (neo-)fundamentalism had become a hermetic movement, closed off to the world and to different schools of Christian thought. Like the original fundamentalists before them, the new post-war evangelicals were also involved in the fight against liberalism and its modernist historical-critical approach to the Bible. The main theological task of evangelicalism (also sometimes called neo-evangelicalism[44]) was to protect the authority of the Bible against the attacks of critics who questioned both its historical accuracy and its uniqueness as inspired revelation.[45]

Evangelicalism, however, was "broader and deeper than any one movement or school," seeking as it did to "relate the historic evangelical faith to current needs and problems in the church and in the wider society."[46] Thus, for example, evangelicalism has been known for its interest in the relationship between science and faith (e.g., Bernard Ramm), as well as a guarded openness to fellowship with non-conservative evangelical Christians (e.g., Billy Graham).[47] Indeed, as has already been mentioned, the movement was founded on the desire to "take to the streets" without,

---

43. Tidball, "Post-War Evangelical Theology," 145.

44. As I am taking a broad view of evangelicalism, I was tempted to title this subsection "Neo-evangelicalism" in order to stress that the group I present is but a subsection of wider evangelicalism. In the end, I decided to bracket "Neo" to avoid potentially limiting the group in many readers' minds to the first, post-war generation of evangelicals. Given the contemporary scene, another possibility for a title could have been "Non Charismatic/Pentecostal Evangelicals," but that assumes too much and seems to minimize the seminal influence post-war evangelicalism has had on charismatic, Pentecostal, and even liberal theologies (and vice versa). For these reasons and others, I have decided to refer to the group I describe in this subsection simply as evangelicals, with the bracketed "Neo" in the title to remind us of the complexities involved in naming the movement.

45. Tidball, "Post-War Evangelical Theology," 149.

46. Bloesch, *Future of Evangelical Christianity*, 30. Roger Olson reminds us that Bloesch has a wide view of evangelicalism, making it essentially a synonym to the totality of that sector of twentieth-century Protestantism, which highlighted the gospel and resisted the subversive forces of secularism and political ideologies. Others, however, hold to a much narrower definition. See Olson, "Locating Bloesch in the Evangelical Landscape," 22.

47. Conn, *Contemporary World Theology*, 127–28.

however, compromising the historic faith. Among other things, this meant being more theologically progressive than fundamentalism had been and also developing a greater sense of ethical responsibility in society.

According to historian Roger Olson, from the beginning, evangelicalism has been divided into two blocs. Olson has called one bloc "traditionalist" and the other "reformist." Olson claims that the difference between the two is not so much a matter of belief or doctrine as of mentality.[48] This partition will prove to complicate matters as we seek to plot the doctrinalist/experientialist divide within evangelicalism.

According to Olsen, the *traditionalist* evangelical values the biblical interpretations and theological formulations of the tradition as normative and binding.[49] In most cases, the "tradition" is traceable to some thread of Princeton theology. Inheriting a defensive position from Princeton and fundamentalism, traditionalists tend to be suspicious of doctrinal revisions and new proposals that may arise from constructive theological reflection. Like their predecessors, they perceive theology essentially as an apologetic task aimed at defending the faith against the wiles of the theologies of the "left." In today's postliberal and postmodern contexts, this means protesting relativistic and pluralistic tendencies wherever they might be found. Evangelical *reformists* also seek to preserve the basic evangelical model and to work within it. But while traditionalists try to preserve the content handed down to them by their theological ancestors in pristine form, reformists engage in a constructive or renewal theology, and for this reason reformists are more open to the arguments of non-evangelicals, believing that there is still "new light" that can shine from the immutable word of God.[50]

Digging deeper into evangelicalism's history, one quite easily finds both doctrinalist and experientialist veins. Attempts to determine where to put down the boundaries, however, can be frustrating. This becomes especially difficult once we realize that apportioning the evangelical landscape between doctrinalists and experientialists does not neatly coincide with Olson's map charting the territories of traditionalists and reformists.

---

48. Olson, "A Forum," 41. Today, these two factions are sometimes described in terms of "conservative" and "postconservative" or simply the "evangelical right" and the "evangelical left." I have followed Olson's distinction because in my opinion it adequately captures the essence of the division without compromising the distinctly evangelical aspects of both camps. Moreover, neither of the terms in Olson's usage carries with it a derogatory connotation.

49. Ibid.

50. Ibid.

Doctrinalism and Experientialism in the Evangelical Tradition

On the one hand, traditionalist evangelicals tend to be more scholastic in their approach to the faith than reformists are, inasmuch as they are more dogmatically bound by the doctrines inherited from Princeton. On the other hand, reformists take a wider stance both in their theological views and in scope and therefore should be, at least in principle, more open to pietist contributions to theology and spirituality. No sooner is the distinction made, however, than we find ourselves overwhelmed by the complexity of the interrelatedness between and the overlapping of the historical and theological data.

One possible way to classify the information might be to make a net distinction between evangelicals derived from the revivalist legacy and those whose roots are in the doctrinalist tradition of Princeton theology.[51] This claim, however, only makes the task of classification even more complicated, for there are traditionalists who have a strong pietist pedigree. Some of these are of the Armenian mold (solidarity with the spirituality of the Wesleyan tradition), while others are Calvinists (guardians of the Puritan inheritance). Both of these groups would be more open to certain revivalist claims and methods than would those traditionalists fixed on perspectives, methodologies, and goals deriving strictly from Princeton scholasticism. Despite evangelical openness to revivalist currents and the greater manifestations of the Spirit sometimes associated with the Holiness movement and its progeny, these evangelicals remain firmly anchored in the Reformation principle of *sola scriptura* as well as the Princeton understanding of the infallibility and inerrancy of the Bible.[52] They adhere faithfully to the grammatical historical method of exegesis, and tend to maintain low-profile worship services compared with those of Pentecostals and charismatics, for example. While some of these evangelical communities have inherited anti-intellectual streaks from neo-fundamentalism (usually the Armenian branch), they are often (but not always) open to interaction with society in general, especially when it concerns works of mercy. Despite the pietist-revivalist influence, these evangelicals maintain a doctrinalist-apologetic approach when it comes to defending the faith, the Bible, and their ecclesial customs.

---

51. Olson, "Locating Bloesch in the Evangelical Landscape," 21.

52. We might point to someone like D. Martyn Lloyd Jones, a staunch Calvinist who preached a doctrine of the baptism of the Holy Spirit. See Lloyd-Jones, *Joy Unspeakable*. See also Andrew Murray, a Calvinist associated with Keswick, and his oft-reprinted book, *The Full Blessing of Pentecost*.

DOCTRINE AND EXPERIENCE

Traditionalists from strictly doctrinalist provenience, however, are the true children of Princeton, and in this respect can be called "rationalists," even if they are open to dialogue with the modern anti-rationalist philosophies.[53] This bloc tends to be predominantly Calvinistic in its theology, and in principle is suspicious of neo-pietism in all its forms. This is quite different, however, from the traditionalism of figures like Martyn Lloyd-Jones or John Piper, who were both staunchly Reformed in their theology but have nevertheless maintained that experience has a central place in Christian life.[54] The traditionalist-doctrinalists, on the other hand, tend to have very strong reservations of any forms of Christianity that place too much emphasis on experiences.[55] While allowing for an experiential aspect of the faith, these doctrinalists tilt heavily towards the rationalist pole of the spectrum, claiming that the scientific study of the Bible should drive Christian spirituality, rather than the other way around. It is important to note that these emphases do not necessarily spring from a disproportionate celebration of human reason, as in rationalism proper. Rather, they stem from the belief that God has given us a Bible whose content is clear enough to be understood adequately with the aid of common sense by any normally functioning intellect (the doctrine of the perspicuity of Scripture). As divine revelation, the Bible is sufficient in itself to solve all eventualities of the Christian life. There is nothing to add to its infallible excellence, and thus it is dishonoring to go in search of God elsewhere—such as, for example, in the realm of our fallible experiences.

Like the Princeton theologians before them, evangelical doctrinalists also tend to reduce the full scope of God's word to the Bible. In so doing, and despite protests, they appear to uphold a hermeneutic more in line with *intelligo ut credam* ("I understand in order to believe") than with its ancient

---

53. See Bloesch, *Future of Evangelical Christianity*, 30. NB: Millard Erickson, who I would place in the above category, criticizes Bloesch for never defining what he means by the term "rationalism" (Erickson, "Donald Bloesch's Doctrine of Scripture," 90–93). For a rebuttal, see Bloesch, "Donald Bloesch Responds," 189–192.

54. At the same time, however, Lloyd-Jones warned that experiences must always be under the authority of the teachings of Scripture and not the other way around (Lloyd-Jones, *Joy Unspeakable*, 16ff.). Piper, a continuist concerning the spiritual gifts, would claim the same.

55. Interesting in this regard is an open letter by Lloyd-Jones' successor at Westminster Chapel, R. T. Kendall, to John MacArthur refuting the latter's comments that Lloyd-Jones was a cessationist who, apparently, would have agreed with the recent Strange Fire conference denunciation of many of the experiences of the Holy Spirit touted by charismatic Christians. See Kendell, "Dear Dr. MacArthur."

cousin statement, *credo ut intelligam* ("I believe in order to understand"). In following this basic hermeneutical principle, however, these evangelicals deviate from the view generally held both by the Fathers of the church and the Reformers themselves.

As is always the case with survey-type analyses, the situation is much more complex then what I have been able to put down on paper. Indeed, doctrinalists could cogently argue that all this is nothing more than a caricature of their position. To a certain extent, it is true, insofar as framing history with words and concepts is essentially an impressionist endeavor in which a selective number of historical facts are brushed onto the canvass to give one picture or another. If we view the portrait from afar, it may well seem to capture reality adequately, but once we move closer, we see it is merely an organized number of dots and slashes that do not so much form a photograph of how things are as a representation according to the artist's juxtaposition of the data. Notwithstanding the element of caricature that is bound to distinguish our picture of evangelical doctrinalism, we can nevertheless affirm through observation that the greatest number of complaints that Christianity is too dry, too rationalist, and lacking in vitality and in warm relationship with God emanate most frequently from doctrinalist camps. These complaints can be seen as symptomatic of what Lloyd-Jones famously called "dead orthodoxy."[56]

Just as it has often happened throughout the history of the church, so also in our time believers, churches, denominations, and movements have stood up in protest against an intellect-dominated, scholastic-leaning Christianity. Objections now, as in the past, are born of the desire for a knowledge of God that is more deeply felt, immediately experienced, and personally significant that reaches beyond reason's ability to master doctrine.

This "felt need" is expressed both within traditionalist and reformist circles. In the former, there is an enduring interest from a Reformed perspective in revivalism,[57] spiritual formation,[58] and a doctrinally informed biblical personalism.[59] Reformists, on the other hand, have gone a step further. Their efforts to overcome dead orthodoxy not only extend to the practical, devotional level, but also to the theological and philosophical.

---

56. Lloyd-Jones, *Revival*, 68–72.
57. E.g., Hansen and Woodbridge, *A God-Sized Vision*.
58. E.g., Carson, *A Call to Spiritual Reformation*; Piper, *A Hunger for God*.
59. E.g., Packer, *Knowing God*.

DOCTRINE AND EXPERIENCE

Whereas traditionalists, for the most part, are content to toe the Princeton line when it comes to the question of the nature and interpretation of Scripture as well as the established expressions of Christian dogma, reformists are much more hermeneutically ecumenical and adventurous and therefore are far less opposed to reexamining and re-contextualizing the older doctrinal formulations.[60] This difference in approach has given rise to yet another way of classifying or dividing evangelicals—namely, as conservatives or postconservatives.

The approach to the Bible of evangelical postconservative reformers such as Clark Pinnock, N. T. Wright, Alister McGrath, Kevin Vanhoozer, Stanley Grenz, Joel Green, and James K. A. Smith, is the result of a fundamental shift in epistemology with respect to their traditionalist colleagues. Postconservative reformers are much more accepting of ways of knowing in general and of knowing God specifically that move beyond the conservative's insistence on the priority of propositional knowledge—i.e., "knowing that." Abandoned are the privileged status of sense data (empirical) and the primacy of reason (theoretical) for coming to know God and God's ways. Added to these, and of no less consequence, are experiential, personal, practical, ethical, sapiential, mystical, and aesthetic ways of knowing. Postconservative reformers therefore denounce all forms of scholasticism. This is not done principally on devotional but rather on epistemological and hermeneutical grounds. In this way, albeit with some sophisticated twists, postconservative evangelicalism has added its voice to the centuries-long conflict between doctrine and experience.[61]

Whether postconservative reformers or open-minded conservative traditionalists, evangelicals are paying more attention to the non-rational dimension of faith. This seems to suggest that a spirituality that reduces knowledge of God to the proposition, is simply insufficiently "real" for many today. Perhaps the most convincing demonstration that a doctrinalist faith is fast becoming less and less persuasive, however, is the exodus

---

60. See for example the Theological Interpretation of Scripture movement, with its "Magna Carta" text, Kevin J. Vanhoozer et al., *Dictionary for Theological Interpretation of the Bible*.

61. On the Anglo-American scene, there is no lack of conservative evangelical material opposing postconservative positions. See, for example, Wells, *No Place for Truth*; Groothuis, *Truth Decay*; Erickson, *Postmodernizing the Faith*; ibid., *Evangelical Left*. For postconservative critiques of the rationalist tendencies of traditional conservative evangelicalism, see Grenz and Franke, *Beyond Foundationalism*; Grenz, *Renewing the Center*; Raschke, *Next Reformation*; Hauerwas, *Unleashing the Scripture*.

of many historic churches from a predominantly rationalist approach to a more enthusiastic one. Historically speaking, this "migration" can perhaps be explained—at least in part—by the widespread perception that charismatic spirituality is somehow better equipped to help believers approach the reality of a living, omnipotent, and glorious God in today's postconservative, postmodern world.

THE CHARISMATIC MOVEMENT

For all their differences, both the Holiness movement and the first Pentecostals shared a common ethos: the desire to go beyond the basic elements of Reformed scholasticism and its emphasis on justification to a more practical Christianity based above all on sanctification understood as a distinct experience realized by the baptism of the Spirit.[62] The charismatic movement was born in the same atmosphere in Van Nuys, California, in 1960, when an Episcopal priest named David Bennett, after conducting a prolonged series of studies on the spiritual life with a small group from his church, informed the congregation on Easter Sunday that he had received the baptism of the Holy Spirit and was speaking in tongues. Many in the congregation did not receive the news with enthusiasm, and in the same year, Bennett resigned from his position as priest.[63]

It was in this way that Pentecostalism first entered into traditional churches. It was big news. This second Pentecostal "wave" quickly spread to other mainline Protestant denominations, and by the mid-60s it had even penetrated the Catholic Church and a number of Orthodox communities in the United States. Unlike Pentecostals, charismatics did not pull away from their denominations but retained their existing confessional membership and loyalty. In other words, opposition to the charismatic upwelling was an inter-confessional matter that involved longtime members of congregations defending their more rationalist brand of Christianity against the intrusive threat of the Pentecostal approach, which was marked by a personal experience of the baptism of the Holy Spirit.[64]

A rapid growth was assisted in the sixties and seventies by the youth-oriented "Jesus People" movement in the United States, and then again in

---

62. It is to be noted that unlike Pentecostals, not all associated with the Holiness movement believed that baptism with the Spirit was an experience added onto justification.

63. Stetzer, "Understanding the Charismatic Movement."

64. See Hocken, "Pentecostal-Charismatic Movement," 36.

a decisive way in the eighties by the so-called "third wave." The third wave was characterized by "a vigorous, independent network of Charismatic churches and organizations" primarily associated with the Vineyard Christian Fellowship founded by John Wimber in California and then with the Toronto and Pensacola revivals.[65] Its range of distinct characteristics can be helpfully summed up by looking at its evangelistic approach, known as "power evangelism." Power evangelism is a missionary strategy that presents the Christian message as viable by virtue of the "powers" it manifests in the lives of believers: healings, miracles, and the ability to cast out the demons that are presented as responsible for most of the ills of world.[66] Another offspring of this third wave is the "Word of Faith Movement" and its theology of prosperity founded by the disciples of Essek William Kenyon (1867–1948), a supporter of the New Thought that issued out of Emerson College of Oratory in Boston.[67] Guided by figures such as Kenneth Hagin, Kenneth Copeland, and, more recently, Benny Hinn, the movement sustains a Christian philosophy based on a theology of positive confession: "What I confess [faith] I possess."

In an attempt to reconcile charismatics and evangelicals, David Pawson has urged each group to benefit from what the other has to teach, as well as to learn from their excesses. For Pawson, a charismatic, such reciprocity would bring about a "fourth-wave."[68] This proposal has given rise to what is called the "post-charismatic critique," which is aimed at separating what is really of the Holy Spirit and what is useless or even harmful to charismatic theology and practice.[69] Despite such a critical self-evaluation from important people within the movement, at the practical and popular levels the movement continues to operate based largely on the characteristics of the second and third waves.

By deliberately emphasizing the baptism of the Spirit, the miraculous gifts, power evangelism, and (sometimes) a gospel of prosperity, the charismatic movement distinguishes itself from the spirituality of both its evangelical and Pentecostal forebearers. Indeed, ever-rarer among charismatics is the cross-centered, daily dying model of sanctification as a way to spiritual growth; it has largely been replaced by a notion of what we might call

65. Eskridge, "Pentecostalism and the Charismatic Movement."
66. Introvigne and Zoccatelli, "La terza ondata: (a)."
67. Introvigne and Zoccatelli, "La terza ondata: (b)."
68. See esp., Pawson, *Fourth Wave*.
69. See, for example, McAlpine, *Post-Charismatic?*

a "positively positive spirituality," which understands spirituality in terms of what the Holy Spirit adds to the believer's essential salvation: more faith, more power, more gifts, more holiness, and so on. That such "additions" to our salvation are generally perceived as occurring in particularly intense "moments" of liberation is yet another indication of the overturn of the idea of disciplined living as a path to spiritual growth. The adoption of this model of spirituality has resulted in a gospel whose emphasis has shifted from what God has done in Christ to what the Holy Spirit did in the New Testament church.

This paradigm shift is a critique not merely of rationalist evangelicalism, but of historic Protestantism itself. It is, among other things, a logical progression of the Pentecostal protest of the Christian faith understood as a mere mental assent to what the Bible says. At the same time, it is also a rebuke of the various pietist and revivalist strains, including the Pentecostalism from which it originated, for not having gone far enough in eradicating doctrinalism and establishing an experientialist model grounded in pneumatic manifestations of the power of the kingdom of God available to the church today.

If charismatics were like earlier experientialist groups that emphasized the supernatural manifestations of the Spirit, it would not have been necessary to write this chapter or even this book. History reveals that both inside and outside of the church there have always been people, groups, and/or movements that have adopted charismatic beliefs and lifestyles.[70] It was not until the onset of the contemporary Pentecostal-charismatic tradition, however, that this particular approach to faith was able to establish itself as a major player in the Christian world. What is original to the con-

---

70. In ancient times, the practice of speaking in unintelligible languages during religious ecstasy was not unknown. In eleventh-century BC Egypt, there was already evidence of ecstatic speech; in the Greek world, the prophetess of Delphi and the Sibylline priestess spoke in unknown tongues. Among the Roman mystery religions, the Dionysian cult was known for this practice. Inside the church, we find the Montanist movement of the second century AD, which boasted of new revelations, prophecies, and speaking in tongues. During the Middle Ages, speaking in tongues was reported in the monasteries of the Orthodox Church. In the Anabaptist Reformation and especially during the Münster revolt, we read of several prophetic deviations that turned out to be catastrophic. In the seventeenth century, it seems that glossolalia had been carried out in France amongst the Huguenots (Protestants) and the Jansenists (Catholic pietists). In the nineteenth century, speaking in tongues was practiced in America amongst the Shakers and Mormons and in Scotland and London among the followers of Edward Irving, who saw the phenomenon as the latter rain of the Holy Spirit before the premillennial return of the Lord.

temporary Pentecostal-charismatic trajectory is that for the first time in history, a restoration movement that sustains a return to the miraculous and charismatic aspects of the New Testament church has actually become big enough to challenge the traditional churches on a global scale.[71]

With respect to this last point, only time will tell if the Spirit of God has called the church in our time to forcefully rediscover the experiences of New Testament believers, to experience the "latter rain" of God's redemptive plan, or whether what we are witnessing in the charismatic movement is largely a social-ecclesial phenomena that has found fertile soil in the contemporary milieu for its mass dissemination. My suspicion is that like all Christian movements that have enjoyed a worldwide growth, the charismatics movement is no different in that it could never have experienced such worldwide success had it not taken root in the historical context in which we presently live. Indeed, over the last two hundred years experientialist approaches have flowered in many areas of life, not only in the church.

In the West, for example, there was the important philosophical, artistic, musical, and literary movement called Romanticism, which opposed the rationalist values and principles of classicism and the Enlightenment. In an illuminating summary in the *Encyclopædia Britannica* online, we read the following.

> Romanticism can be seen as a rejection of the precepts of order, calm, harmony, balance, idealization, and rationality that typified Classicism in general and late eighteenth-century Neoclassicism in particular. It was also to some extent a reaction against the Enlightenment and against eighteenth-century rationalism and physical materialism in general. Romanticism emphasized the individual, the subjective, the irrational, the imaginative, the personal, the spontaneous, the emotional, the visionary, and the transcendental.[72]

Closer to our time, there are the formidable Hegelian, existentialist, and postmodernist philosophical critiques of the "oppressive rationalist regimes" of the preceding worldviews, as well as the modern and postmodern

---

71. Over the course of half a century, charismatic Christianity, with its doctrines of baptism and the gifts of the Holy Spirit, has surpassed both Pentecostals and evangelicals in terms of worldwide adherents. According to a 2011 survey by the Pew Research Forum, there are 279,080,000 Pentecostals worldwide, 285,480,000 evangelicals, and 304,990,000 charismatics (Street et al., *Global Christianity*).

72. *Encyclopædia Britannica Online*, s.v. "Romanticism."

uprisings in art, literature, music, and architecture, all of which combine to universally contest the orderly and calculated past to promote an openness to a more chaotic or, in any case, an experience-based future. Moreover, we must consider the "liberating" and introspective influences of Freudian psychology, Eastern mystical religion, and New Age thought that the post-war, anti-establishment generations have embraced to one degree or another in the West. All these modes and movements have helped give rise to what we might paradoxically call a "grassroots elitism," in which the "commoner" is encouraged to seek power through freedom from the restrictions of previous oppressive formulas, laws, and doctrines. The final objective is that each person be allowed to autonomously manage his or her own life, unbridled from slavery to the canons of reason, logic, tradition, and even common sense (i.e., Enlightenment values). In short, the charismatic movement was born in a cultural environment ripe for an exuberant, anti-dogmatic, freedom-loving "religion of the Spirit."

Of course, our ability to place the charismatic movement within a historical framework does not invalidate it as a genuine work of God's Spirit any more than being able to determine the various subtexts of Second Temple Judaism in first-century Judea annuls the divine legitimacy of the birth of the Christian Way. On the other hand, neither the explosive worldwide spread of charismatic practice nor the zeal of its adherents is a guarantee that it is of God. Perhaps this would not even be an issue were it not for the spectacular claims of uniqueness that Pentecostals and charismatics often make or, in any case, believe about themselves. On historical and theological grounds, there are simply too many question marks for the movement to be embraced uncritically. On the other hand, it is simply too big to dismiss as a fluke.

My own approach would be to wait and see if, like evangelicalism, it can establish itself as an *ecclesia semper reformanda est*—a movement that is continuously reforming itself from within through intensely honest self-criticism. This would mean exposing its theories and practices to the rigors of biblical and theological scrutiny, even if that means in-house bickering and the abandonment of certain received beliefs. On this front, the post-charismatic critique is certainly a good start. Whatever the future might have in store, it would be wise to hold very lightly onto the claim that the charismatic expression of Christianity is either the last great movement of the Spirit in the history of the present age ("the latter rain") or the restoration *par excellence* of long-lost Christian truths and practices.

A more restrained approach would be to understand the charismatic movement—with all its shortcomings—as a wake-up call to a Bible-believing faith that had become so consumed by defending itself against Christian and secular liberalism that it adopted the stringently rationalist and/or empirical mind-set of its adversaries in order to fight them on their own turf. Along the way, however, it forgot that Christianity was meant to be so much more than simply believing that the Bible is without error and infallible. This is not to suggest that charismatics were raised solely as a divine critique of doctrinalist evangelicals—such a claim would be presumptuous. We would do better looking at the situation from the vantage point of the history previewed in this chapter. From this perspective, with its "in your face" approach, charismatic Christianity may be seen as a persistent heckler that nevertheless commands a true voice of its own, standing up in the halls of rationalist religion to mock the "lettered" with shouts of praise and joy unto a living and very active Messiah.[73] As with all heckling, this interruption can annoy those who simply want to get on with the quiet life they have grown accustomed to. On the other hand, it can also degenerate into ungrounded judgments of those who rightfully refuse to surrender any ground whatsoever when it comes to the centrality of true doctrine for a genuine, living faith.

Perhaps we are to understand the current situation as a case of iron sharpening iron, in which through sheer force and persistence, doctrinalists have had no choice but to stand up and take notice that theirs is indeed a glorious God who desires above all else to be glorified through his living presence in and amongst his people of all ages. Nevertheless, it still needs to be seen if charismatic Christianity will stop seeing itself as the one doing all the sharpening in order to allow the Spirit of God to use others to do some much-needed sharpening on them as well.

POSTSCRIPT: HOW HISTORY HUMBLES US

One of the most useful aspects of studying the history of the church is its humility factor. If read with an open mind, ecclesial history humbles us, demonstrating that no one institution, denomination, movement, or theological current can boast of having the perfect knowledge of God or the perfect way of knowing God. For this reason, neither can any one group

---

[73] For a philosophical treatment of the contribution of a Pentecostal worldview, see Smith, *Thinking in Tongues*.

claim to practice the one true Christian spirituality unless it has a proper sense of balance between Christian doctrine and experience.

I firmly believe that Scripture is the sure guide in these matters, but this is also part of the problem, insofar as different traditions interpret the Bible differently and are selective in choosing which Scriptures get most attention. In tracing the history of conflict between the poles of doctrinalism and experientialism, I think this became apparent. By bringing this matter into focus, it was my hope to provide a historical framework that would allow us to more judiciously evaluate the various notions and practices of spirituality circuiting the current evangelical scene as it is broadly conceived.

The multifaceted reality of how God works through history to achieve his objectives must be the subject of another book. Nevertheless, we can say at least one thing based on our historical survey: in God's providence in raising up particular groups of Christians to do his will at certain times in history, each group is so closely tied to its historical and cultural contexts that it seems inconceivable to think any one of them could have arisen at any other time or in any other series of contexts. This was true for the various expressions of Christianity in the first century, and it is true for us today.

God's truth, I believe, is truth for all ages and in all situations; nevertheless, how that truth is interpreted and practiced is inextricably tied to one's place in history and in the world. Pluralism is a fact. We need to deal with it honestly if we love God's truth. Having said this, I also believe that truth is by nature resilient, so that it is able to adapt its essence to differing historical forms without being any less true. This would seem to have to be the case, given the dialectical nature of God in his act of revealing himself. That is to say, God has sometimes revealed himself as a paradox.[74] Many a historical conflict has derived from the antinomies of God, including, I would submit, the one I have just examined between doctrinalist and experientialist expressions of faith. It is precisely because of the dialectical dimension of truth, therefore, that we should always exercise humble

---

74. This may be seen by examining how some of his divine attributes appear to flatly contradict each other. For example, how can his mercy and justice coexist without turning him into a schizophrenic deity? Or how can he be completely transcendent while at the same time be so intimately connected to human beings within the confines of history? How is it possible that he is perfect in his pureness and yet for a time tolerates a sinful world? And what about a God who is spirit suffering in the flesh? To assume perfect clarity of the divine paradoxes can be considered nothing short of presumption.

caution before claiming our community or group has recovered the one true, universally binding statement of New Testament or any other historically-situated Christianity.[75]

Indeed, it is debatable whether it is even desirable to return to a former time, since that temporal segment is gone forever. To be faithful to the living Christ is to be faithful to him where *we live*, not where others have toured before us. Of course, imitation of Christ and of the great saints is part of our Christian heritage; nevertheless, we need to stand guard lest imitation mutate into mere impersonation or, worse, pretense. The Lord has given us a map of the terrain travelled by the first-century church, plus a sufficient body of revelation to ensure successive generations need not start at ground zero every time. There are points on that map that have eternal and universal properties (e.g., Christ's forgiveness, the outpouring of the Holy Spirit, the revelation of such events) and others that were and remain historically conditioned (e.g., the particular events surrounding Pentecost, the problems at Corinth and Galatia, a definitive liturgy).

To help the church navigate, the Father sent his Holy Spirit, who is our living compass. But the Spirit is a free Person and not a mechanical contraption bound to the laws of magnetism. For this reason, each new generation would do well to seek with all its might to know both the divine atlas inscribed in human symbols mapping out once for all proper doctrine for the church *and* the personal Spirit, who helps us interpret not only Scripture, but also our own historically conditioned life-situations according to truth—and all this so that we might walk in light and love. To help us see more clearly and love each other more intensely, however, we would also do well to grow in the awareness that our congregation, our denomination, our movement, and even our mind-set have not fallen directly from heaven into our local neighborhood but are rather concretely and irreversibly circumscribed by the times we live in, the place we occupy, the choices we make, and the preferences we have.

Unfortunately, what we often find among believers is the conviction that they have received once and for all the divine implications and applications of Scripture, the perfectly worked-out understanding of a doctrine, or the irrefutable voice of God for this or that historically-conditioned matter. Should we be inclined to think that good, solid, historic-grammatical

---

75. For a brief but penetrating demonstration of the impossibility of having direct or, in any case, unmediated access to the apostolic witness of Christ, see Holmes, *Listening to the Past*, 7–8.

exegesis of the Bible would solve all these conflicts, even a cursory glance at the field of biblical studies is sufficient to discover that there are no less enduring conflicts here than in the more speculative theologies.[76] On the other hand, should we deny or even take lightly the diligent study of those same Scriptures, it would be better that we had never been born. Similarly, we are warned by those same Scriptures to not quench the Spirit or despise prophecy.

To deny that our particular voicing of the faith is at the same time a locus plotted on a historical map—a set of points satisfying the conditions of the tradition in which we find ourselves—is tantamount to refuting that who I am has been conditioned by where I was born and reared, who my parents, siblings, teachers and friends have been, my body type, my psychological and biological constitutions, my experiences, and my hopes and fears. Am I more than the sum of my parts? I believe so, but at the same time, I am not less than that sum. So it is with our particular expression of Christian faith and spirituality. The Christian faith is greater than the sum of its situated parts, for its author is Christ; nevertheless, in practice it is always conditioned by an incalculable number of factors, so that it never rises completely above its historical situatedness. The guidebook is divinely and unalterably revealed truth. And a good thing it is too, because the way any one person, community, denomination, or movement puts it into practice is bound to be full of gaps. To think otherwise is to fall into the "sin" of modernity—the presumption that we are able to grab hold of reality *as it is in itself*, as if dropped from the God-sphere into our own personal histories.

Truth for us, therefore, is to a degree always *truth-as-we-experience it* in our embodied existence. Human reason does indeed have a formidable capacity for transcendence, but it remains nonetheless markedly burdened by any number of cognitive, psychological, cultural, historical, and even physiological influences brought to bear on it. Or perhaps we should not even be speaking in terms of limitations; perhaps it is simply God's good intention for created humanity that we sharpen and broaden our capacity for understanding truth through the very struggles we have witnessed in our examination of church history—struggles that, when worked through with godly humility are designed to make us wise unto the building up of our character into Christ-likeness.[77]

76. For a book advancing this thesis, see Adam, *Faithful Interpretation*.

77. For the thesis that creational situatedness is not the result of the fall but is rather "built into" God's good creation, see Smith, *Fall of Interpretation*.

DOCTRINE AND EXPERIENCE

It is in this spirit, therefore, that I proceed to tackle the question of doctrine and experience as it relates to spirituality in the contemporary evangelical world.

Chapter 2

Bibliolatry
Making Idols of the Words of God

I consider the brief historical survey of the previous chapter important for at least three reasons. First, it underscores the humility needed when critically appraising doctrinalist and experientialist tendencies within the church. Second, examination of the perennial conflict between doctrinalism and experientialism in the church provides a historical setting in which to insert the present situation. Third, the theological development of the clash between doctrinalism and experientialism provides fodder for the formulation of an informed thesis for understanding the conflict within contemporary evangelicalism.

The first part of this thesis is that the rise of experientialism in all its various manifestations is a symptom of a malady in the broader evangelical movement today—namely, a top-heavy desire to break free from the perceived constrictions of doctrine in order to know God spiritually. I will deal with this aspect in the next chapter. The second part of the thesis is that, just as the original Pietism of the seventeenth and eighteenth centuries was a helpful (though sometimes extreme) equalizer to the doctrinalism of the early Protestant scholastics, the neo-pietism that characterizes many evangelical churches today is also a legitimate though often exaggerated critique of a rationalistic and/or scientific orthodoxy practiced within traditional evangelicalism.[1]

---

1. For the term and description of "neo-pietism," see Bloesch, *God, Authority, and*

DOCTRINE AND EXPERIENCE

The experientialist reaction of our time is the result of more than a century-and-a-half of a traditional evangelicalism that has believed the main task of the church in the world is to provide a rational defense (*apologia*) of the Bible and its content.[2] In line with the other manifestations of rationalism in Christian history, this approach also tends to encapsulate faith into a mental assent to a body of biblical doctrines rightly understood. It is to this perceived problem that I now turn my attention.

INTRODUCTION TO BIBLIOLATRY

> This is what I mean by the end of doctrine: it has come to an end when it cannot by definition say anything new and when the sole measurement of doctrine's significance is its contribution as the authoritative enforcer of the church's identity.[3]

> Although charismatics have given a higher priority to experience than to relationship, rationalistic evangelicals have given a higher priority to knowledge than to relationship . . . This emphasis on knowledge over relationship has produced in us a bibliolatry.[4]

Evangelical doctrinalists tend to be skeptical of the search for a more "felt" faith. This is an understandable reaction when we consider the excesses that often arise when experiences and feelings are inordinately emphasized in our relationship with God. There is, however, also a sense in which the skepticism of doctrinalism is irrational according to its own canons of reason.

Doctrinalists correctly maintain that the Bible is the final standard of teaching, correction, and training for the Christian faith (2 Tim 3:16). They traditionally pay meticulous attention to hermeneutical and exegetical methods and details for assurance that they are rightly dividing the word of truth (2 Tim 2:15). They refuse to budge on both the fundamental and central importance of the Bible for the Christian spiritual life. However, such firmness sometimes turns into stubbornness and, similarly, the love of

---

Salvation, 1. "Scientism" is characterized by having an exaggerated confidence in the principles and methods of science.

2. Harris, *Fundamentalism and Evangelicals*, 100. Harris underscores that evangelicals tend to think like this, notwithstanding the concomitant belief that human reason must submit itself to the revelations of Scripture.

3. Helmer, *Theology and the End of Doctrine*, 7.

4. Wallace, "Uneasy Conscience of a Non-Charismatic Evangelical."

truth regresses into an unconscious infatuation with a limited canon of biblical doctrines related to the confession of a certain theological tradition. In these cases, the study of the Bible is never far removed from the apologetic task of defending one's particular creed. In this way, the Book of Christ is in constant risk of being revered above the Christ of the Book.

When doctrinalists hear statements like this last one, they naturally recoil. This reaction is due to the ruling assumption doctrinalists hold that we can only truly know Christ through the Bible. Knowing the Book of Christ is, therefore, identical to knowing the Christ of the Book and even precedes it. But the thesis of doctrinalism appears to be contested by the very same Bible, for there are numerous passages therein signifying possibilities for knowing God without Bible in hand, though this is not the same as saying that the word of God is absent. We will return to this notion later.

To my mind, the increasing emphasis on the search for the personal presence of God in all the church's functions, from worship service to business meetings, is a welcome return to a pneumatic emphasis perhaps too often overlooked in the traditional evangelical world. The invocation of the glory, the majesty, and power of God has its roots firmly in the practice of both mosaic Israel and the new covenant church.

Concentrating on the New Testament, Paul, for example, prayed that believers might receive a spirit of wisdom and revelation from heaven so that they might know the fullness of the "Father of glory" and that they might be enlightened in order to know the "riches of his glorious inheritance in the saints" and "immeasurable greatness of his power" (Eph 1:17–19). Peter wrote of how we rejoice "with joy that is inexpressible and filled with glory," though we have yet to see the Lord (1 Pet 1:8), and also of his "divine power," which he has entrusted to us (2 Pet 1:3). The writer of Hebrews made reference to the pneumatic realities experienced even by eventual apostates who had been enlightened, had "tasted the heavenly gift," and had "shared in the Holy Spirit," having "tasted the goodness of the word of God and the powers of the age to come" (Heb 6:4–5). Once again, Paul spoke of the believer "with unveiled face, beholding the glory of the Lord . . . being transformed" into the image of Christ from glory to glory, by the Lord, who is the Spirit (2 Cor 3:18). Finally, we have the practice of the first disciples in imitation of Jesus praying to God as "Abba, Father" (Rom 8:15; Gal 4:6; cf. Mark 14:36), indicating the high level of personal intimacy with God that believers can have and must seek with all their capacities (Jer

29:13; Luke 11:9).[5] At face value, these examples cannot all be interpreted as statements of positional sanctification or future eschatology; they surely refer to the Christian's present-day experience of God.

Furthermore, we find a genuine pneumatic-linguistic phenomenon in the Scriptures that is admittedly sometimes difficult to accept in lieu of the many abuses found in certain Christian environments concerning the direct guidance of the Holy Spirit. However, it is a way of speaking that apparently was not at all scandalous for a church that had just experienced the promised outpouring of the Holy Spirit (Acts 2:4) and subsequent fillings of the same (e.g., Acts 4:31). There was also the prescriptive realized eschatological instruction to walk according to the Spirit (Gal 5:16; cf. Eph 5:18), who gives Christ's very life to believers (Rom 8:10). I refer to speech, apparently common in the early church, such as: "the Spirit said" (Acts 8:29), "the Spirit said to him" (Acts 10:19), "The Spirit told me" (Acts 11:12), "the Holy Spirit said" (Acts 13:2), "having been forbidden by the Holy Spirit" and not allowed "by the Spirit of Jesus" (Acts 16:6, 7), "the Holy Spirit testifies to me" (Acts 20:23), "Thus says the Holy Spirit" (Acts 21:11), "speaking in the Spirit of God" (1 Cor 12:3), "He who has an ear, let him hear what the Spirit says to the churches" (Rev 2:7, 11, 17, 28; 3:6, 13, 22), and so on.

The historical abuses of such "Spirit-talk" remind us of the need to test the spirits to see if they are truly from God (1 John 4:1). Having said this, however, the existence of such abuses should not push us to the other extreme of skepticism concerning the availability of the Spirit of God in these last days to speak to us prophetically in dreams, in visions, or simply in the calm of our spirits (Acts 2: 17–18). Such intimacy seems to be corroborated by the intensely personal relationship with God granted to the true disciple (John 14:20).[6]

Should we wish to envision such communication by the Spirit *above all* in terms of direct audible words from heaven, mass fabricated prophecies, or visions and dreams given to a supposed elite, then it is our loss! Conversely, any disciple who knows Christ (in the sense of personal Johannine *ginosko* and Petrine *epiginosko*) should expect the Spirit to speak in a personal way, even regarding the ordinary things of everyday life. After all, if the Lord in Scripture exhorts us to ask him to pray for wisdom in order

---

5. NB: Contrary to common opinion, the term "Abba" probably is not exactly equivalent with the English appellative "Daddy," because it was also used by disciples in antiquity to refer to a greatly loved and respected master. Nonetheless, it is indeed a familiar term that denotes great intimacy (Dunn, "Prayer," 619–20).

6. I treat this theme more fully in the last section of the present chapter.

to tackle the various trials of this life as Christians (Jas 1:5), where is the scandal if he answers us with a clear word of wisdom in prayer or meditation, through song, a work of art, or even a football game? Similarly, if a servant of the Lord is searching out the divine will concerning the direction his or her ministry is to take, where would be the outrage should the Lord appear in a dream to encourage that servant to seek out the many people in their city who have yet to be reached (Acts 18:10)? Or if we are tired and discouraged in our service or even from the simple struggles of life, especially if it appears we have been abandoned, why should we doubt that God could console us directly in our spirits, in "the sound of a low whisper" (1 Kgs 19:12)?

This does not mean that God reveals himself to his disciples only or even especially in these ways. Surely the Scriptures are the most common way that the Lord speaks to us; after all, the Scriptures are the most complete and "natural" means of divine communication, being God's revelation in intelligible and, for the most part, clear human language. However, it is inaccurate to claim that God speaks *only* in this way, especially if it means that the Lord communicates only through our cognitive processes acting upon the propositions contained within the pages of the Bible.[7]

Nevertheless, there is an alarming evangelical bias towards a rationalist—but also a naturalist or scientistic—model of spirituality we can call "bibliolatry." I do not use this term to refer to those who adhere to narrow or simplistic views of inerrancy, infallibility, or the supremacy of the Bible. This would be the common way of understanding the term "bibliolatry." In the present context, that is simply too general to be useful. Rather, I use it to refer to a methodological source for spirituality that sometimes or perhaps often accompanies those who support these doctrines narrowly defined. Specifically, bibliolatry *identifies propositional knowledge of the Bible as that knowledge of God that is of itself sufficient for uniting us to God in spiritual relationship.*

Propositional knowledge, in this case, is not to identify strictly with the declarative sentences of Scripture. Clearly, evangelicals take seriously all speech-acts found in the Bible, such as promise, inquiry, exhortation, command, and so on. Rather, evangelical propositionalism extends to any affirmation we can make based on any kind of biblical speech. Thus, for

---

7. See George Lindbeck's first of three approaches to doctrine—namely, cognitive-propositionalism, which conceives of doctrine as "propositions or truth claims about objective realities" (Lindbeck, *Nature of Doctrine*, 16).

example, Jesus' command that "you also are to love one another" can be put into the proposition "Jesus commands that we love one another," while the inquiry of the psalmist as to why God is mindful of humanity (Ps 8:4) can be restated as the declarative that God is mindful of us, though we are unworthy of his attention. Indeed, "[t]he main defect of propositionalism is that it reduces the variety of speech actions in the canon to one type: the assertion."[8] This kind of "knowing *that*" is what undergirds the epistemology of bibliolatry.[9]

While propositionalism is a rationalistic theory, in modern thought it has been married (often unwittingly) to empiricism such that true knowledge is understood as the true statements we can make about reality based on what we can determine scientifically. Evangelicals have largely bought into this model, conceiving of biblical knowledge as a parallel to how the natural scientist knows the world and makes true statements about it.[10] For the scientist, one cannot know the natural world without observing, examining, and, finally, interpreting it. The idea is to collect enough of the proper kind of data to make truthful statements about physical reality. Of course, this method has been spectacularly successful in the realm of nature. Unfortunately, what has emerged from such success in much evangelical thought is a general epistemological assumption that any assumed "knowledge" unable to withstand objective, empirical scrutiny does not count as true knowledge because assertions made concerning it are not empirically verifiable. Thus, the kind of "Spirit-talk" alluded to above is discarded out of hand as subjective. Outside the evangelical sphere, some even go so far as to make the ontological claim (based on this model) that all reality is ultimately reducible to the natural world, its laws, and its principles.[11]

Notwithstanding their commitment to supernaturalism, bibliolaters have adopted the modernist's ontology of materiality that defines reality as

8. Vanhoozer, *Drama of Doctrine*, 266.

9. For an extreme example of this view, see Johnson, "Mysticism and Evangelical Thought"; ibid., *Faith Misguided*.

10. For an example, see Hodge, *Systematic Theology*, 1:10.

11. This thought comes from a methodological position known by names such as philosophical materialism, physicalism, or naturalistic reductionism. It claims that everything is physical or material such that everything that is—including mental, religious, moral, and social phenomena—depends on and is rendered necessary by the physical. Therefore, all reality can be studied by the natural sciences. What cannot be studied is not counted as real in an objective sense. For a popular dissemination of this metaphysic in debate with religion, refer to the writings of the New Atheists such as Richard Dawkins, Sam Harris, Daniel Dennett, and the late Christopher Hitchens.

"what can be encountered with the five senses."[12] According to this paradigm, "something exist[s] by virtue of its physical properties."[13] Without physical properties, something simply cannot be said "to be." Moreover, what *is not*, *cannot* be known. In a subtle, yet strikingly similar manner, the bibliolater believes that what we can know of the reality of God is contained wholly within the physical boundaries of the biblical documents, for "Individual (token) sentences are physical entities."[14] No manifestation of God outside the propositions of Scripture can be counted on to provide certain knowledge of God. Therefore, if we are to know God as he really is, such knowledge must come through the "materiality" of the Bible filtered through our human senses and intellectual faculties. Analogously to the naturalistic reductionist's insistence that "true truth" is contained only within the boundaries of the empirically observable physical world, the bibliolater maintains that all that can be truly known about God is located within the pages of the Bible.

The self-revelation of God for bibliolaters is therefore reducible to the linguistic codes engraved in the physical pages of the biblical documents. According to this approach, knowing God is synonymous with properly deciphering the codes of the sacred texts and placing them in their proper location within the greater theological system.[15] Consequently, in principle the bibliolater can claim, "I know God through the Bible, even though I have never had a personal experience of him." Such a statement ironically betrays the similarities cognitive-propositionalism shares with classical natural theology, which claims certain things about God can be known truly through reason acting on creation independently of special revelation. Furthermore, it is not dissimilar to the "extraordinary contention" of the liberal theologian Schubert Ogden, who wrote, "even though faith without theology is not really faith at all, theology without faith is still theology, and quite possibly good theology at that."[16] Crouching behind both of Ogden's theses is the naturalist assumption: cognitive-empirically derived content

---

12. Walton, "Creation in Genesis," 56.

13. Ibid.

14. Hill, "Proposition," 632.

15. "One of the most influential images of theology as a *scientia* of Scripture depicts it as the process of abstracting revealed truths—propositions—from the biblical text and arranging them in logical order" (Vanhoozer, *Drama of Doctrine*, 266).

16. Ogden, *On Theology*, 19, cited in Bloesch, *A Theology of Word and Spirit*, 124.

DOCTRINE AND EXPERIENCE

concerning God is a prerequisite for knowing God, whereas personal experience (i.e., a faith relationship) of God is not.

A sound naturalistic approach to the Scriptures for knowing God clearly has great value, but a problem arises when the theologian, following the scientist, claims that God is knowable exclusively through the cognitive-propositional method applied to the Bible. It is true that God reveals himself to us through the Scriptures, but it is overstating the case to affirm that understanding what the Bible says is equal to knowing God. Such a view cannot see beyond the logical network of biblical language to meet the One who calls us to kneel continually before his throne[17] and not in front of his library.

Once again we affirm that the Scriptures are indeed a special and integral means through which God has revealed himself to us. However, this must not imply that "knowing God" is reducible to "learning the Bible." The Bible itself indicates a living God who also reveals himself through direct revelation (Matt 16:16–17), obedience to his will (John 14:21), prayer (Luke 6:12–13; 9: 28), solitude (Ps 37:7), creation (Ps 19:1–2), the sincere pursuit of him (Jer 29:13), service (Matt 25:40), daily faithfulness (Mal 3:10), fasting (Acts 13:2), visions (Gen 15:1; Acts 9:10), dreams (Gen 20:3; 41:24), and the breaking of bread (Luke 24:35–36). Of course, the knowledge of God we might gain through these revelatory means are not to replace the Bible as the normative basis of our doctrine concerning who God is and what he has done, but neither can we eliminate them offhand as sources from which we gain true spiritual knowledge of God.

My purpose in all this is neither to suggest that we should replace biblical facts, data, and information with a pursuit of experience, nor to argue that the latter is a superior means of knowing God spiritually. Bibliolatry is not in error because it holds the Bible in high esteem as a source of true knowledge of God but rather because it conceives the Bible as the only means of such knowledge. However, this is not even the ultimate cause of the error—that belongs to the belief that the knowledge of God we *can* obtain through the biblical propositions is, as a source, sufficient for Christian spirituality. In the final analysis, it dispenses with the Holy Spirit as the immediate means for knowing God and replaces it with the human intellectual endeavor applied to the sacred texts.[18] As such, it is the veneration of the created over and above the Creator; it is idolatry.

---

17. Raschke, *Next Reformation*, 135.

18. In his canonical-linguistic explanation of the role of doctrine in Christian

Bibliolatry

"WORD OF GOD" AND THE BIBLE

I love the Bible. More accurately, I love the word of God. The two are inseparably bound together, but it is important to make the distinction. The Bible is composed of words, but it is also an expression of God's word. The Bible tells many stories, but it is also the word that is the metanarrative story of God and all existence. The Bible is a collection of ancient documents, but it is also the word that continues to document and inform our present reality.[19]

And this word of God which brought all worlds into being cannot be understood to mean the Bible, for it is not a written or printed word at all, but the expression of the will of God spoken into the structure of all things . . . . The Bible is the written word of God, and because it is written, it is confined and limited by the necessities of ink and paper. The voice of God, however, is alive and free as the sovereign God is free.[20]

The Bible is a legacy left us by God. Its value is literally incalculable for the disciple of Jesus Christ. It is no less than eternal life, insofar as it communicates the words and concepts of Jesus (John 6:68). The Scriptures are wonderful because they can be studied profoundly and extensively for a lifetime without ever exhausting the treasures contained therein. At the same time, the least educated disciple can amply excavate its great depths for all that pertains to true life. It is precisely because the Bible is a book of spiritual words that we should not reduce it to a series of "divine data." While familiarity with the Scriptures is always proposed as a means for discovering the word of God (2 Tim 3:14–17), the Bible itself puts us in contact with various means—other than reading or studying the Scriptures—through which we may come to know God. I listed some of these ways above, as attested by the Bible itself. In what follows, I will expand on them, especially as they relate to the notion of "word of God."

For example, Jesus teaches that "[i]f anyone's will is to do God's will, he will know whether the teaching is from God or whether I am speaking on my own authority" (John 7:17). In this case, it is not the human intellect

---

theology, Kevin Vanhoozer does not believe the criticism that propositionalism overlooks the Holy Spirit is sound (Vanhoozer, *Drama of Doctrine*, 268n10). From a linguistic point of view, I would agree with Vanhoozer. From a purely epistemological perspective, however, I think the critique stands.

19. Hoffman, "Bible as Word of God," 348.
20. Tozer, *Pursuit of God*.

engaged in the study of the Scriptures that enables us to identify the word of God but rather the human *will* directed to the divine will. More specifically, it indicates that our discernment of the true value of the divine words does not ultimately depend on our intellectual ability or method of exegesis but rather on our will to obey God (though where intellect and sound interpretation is lacking, we risk misunderstanding what God's will is for us).

Centuries before, the wise man had said that the beginning of true science is not ultimately reducible to an active intellect but rather to a *pious disposition*—namely, the fear of the Lord (Prov 1:7; 9:10). Hebrew wisdom also asserted that knowing God is the result of a *passion* to seek out God with all one's heart (Prov 2:4–5; cf. Jer 29:13). It is not insignificant that the great theologian and exegete of the New Testament, the Apostle Paul, despite being rigorously trained in the schools of rabbinic exegesis, did not actually hear the word of God until he met the risen Christ on the road to Damascus in what can be described only as a *mystical-existential encounter* (Acts 9:1–18).[21]

From the perspective of the various ways for coming to know God taught in Scripture, it becomes clear that bibliolatry proves unable to provide a method for a complete Christian spirituality. Again, this is not because bibliolatry greatly esteems the Bible but rather because it reduces saving knowledge of God to merely learning the Bible's content and assenting to it. The Scriptures themselves identify a properly directed will, piety, passion, and existential encounter as effective means of knowing the word of the Lord. Indeed, it is arguable whether, without these virtues, the intellect can know the Bible without knowing the word of God, which is living and active (Heb 4:12).

To demonstrate this principle further, we can examine the first verses of Hebrews:

> Long ago, at many times and in many ways, God spoke to our fathers by the prophets, but in these last days he has spoken to us by his Son, whom he appointed the heir of all things, through whom also he created the world. (Heb 1:1–2)

When we read in this passage that God no longer speaks to us through the prophets but through the Son, it surely means that the word of truth spoken by, in, and through Jesus Christ is the fulfillment of the words of God announced and sometimes inscribed by the prophets. In this sense,

---

21. In zealously persecuting the church, perhaps we may deduce that Paul, in his misguided way, had been seeking the Lord with all his heart.

therefore, the Bible is undoubtedly the word of God *written down* for the salvation of all those who obtain eternal life and as a witness against all who do not.

From this vantage point, Karl Barth's hermeneutical assertion that the Bible *becomes* the word of God only when the reader encounters Christ therein is not completely accurate.[22] We can sustain this assertion from a passage like the one below:

> And we also thank God constantly for this, that when you received the word of God, which you heard from us, you accepted it not as the word of men but as what it really is, the word of God, which is at work in you believers. (1 Thess 2:13)

If Paul's preaching was indeed the word of God, and if what he wrote down faithfully reflected what he said in his preaching, it follows that his epistles are to be considered the word of God (and, we might add, all faithful preaching of those Scriptures[23]). Furthermore, if all the biblical documents follow this principle in one way or another—that is, if they are overall divinely revealed Scripture—we can safely deduce that the Bible is, in fact, the word of God.[24]

However, the fact that we always need to qualify "word of God" with adjectival phrases such as "announced publically" or "put into writing" when referring to prophetic preaching and the Scriptures suggests that in some profound sense the word of God transcends its forms in human language. There is indeed a very thin line of demarcation (some would say insignificant) between a "word" and the way in which it is expressed (i.e., spoken or written). The expression of the word of God in First Thessalonians was the message of the gospel. But just as in one sense a message from God is clearly a word of God, in another sense it is less than the word itself because the message in words is the expression of the word but not identical to it. Mark Hoffman synthetically expresses the complex relationship between the Bible and the word of God in the following passage:

---

22. A trend in some recent interpretations of Barth is that the great Swiss theologian also argued that the Bible was in some sense in and of itself the word of God. See, for example, McCormack, "Being of Holy Scripture."

23. This is of course nothing new to classical Reformed thought. In the Second Helvetic Confession, for example, both Scripture and the preaching of Scripture are affirmed to be the true word of God.

24. See Greidanus, "Nature of Paul's Letters."

DOCTRINE AND EXPERIENCE

> The Bible and the word of God are inseparably bound but not identical. The Bible is the best and most reliable witness to the word of God, but the word of God exists independently of and prior to the Bible. If the word of God is like life-giving water, the Bible is not a jar of water but a boat riding on an ever-flowing stream.[25]

With this thought, Hoffman explains that the Bible is not the word of God because it contains within itself divine properties but rather because the divine bears it up. Regardless of whether a boat had ever existed or not, the river would have flowed just the same. The Bible, therefore, does not bring forth the word of God—conversely, it is carried by it! If this is indeed the case, then the word of God is ultimately independent of the Bible, whereas the Bible is completely dependent on the word of God. The Bible is the word of God, but the word of God goes beyond the Bible.

Returning to Heb 1:1–2 (and following), it is clear that the writer of the letter wanted to communicate that in the revelation of the Son, God announced to the world a revolutionary paradigm of existence. With the coming of the Son, the old reality has been superseded by the new in excellence. The fabric of time and space was torn definitively in this event, so that all people, from the greatest to the smallest, could now enjoy the heavenly gift and the good word of God and become partakers of the Holy Spirit, enjoying the powers of the future world (Heb 6:4–5; cf. John 1:9). Though we do not yet know the fullness of this glorious day, surely the future has already entered in the present to some extent. Now even the simplest believer can move beyond the curtain to catch a true glimpse of the glory of God in his Son (Heb 6:19; 10:20). Such knowledge and experience is greater than that known by the greatest prophets of old (Heb 1:1–2; Matt 11:11).

The question that concerns us presently is how we come to know this reality. The answer the writer to the Hebrews gives is: through the word of God. But this gives rise to another question: How are we to understand the word of God in this sense? Is it the Bible, so that we can say that it is sufficient to study, read, listen, and assent to the Old and New Testaments in order to experience the heavenly reality of which the letter to the Hebrews speaks? If we affirm this, are we to conceive of these documents, inspired as they are, as the beginning and end of the matter? Must we not rather admit that the word of God transcends the Bible, with the latter a means rather than an end in itself? In addition to this, if the Bible were to encompass all that the word of God is, would we not be constrained to say that the disciple

---

25. Hoffman, "Bible as Word of God," 348.

is called to obey a written document and not the risen Lord? The Scriptures themselves indicate that we are called to worship God alone and to sit at the feet of his Son, Jesus Christ; to be a slave to any other person or thing is idolatry. If, therefore, the word of God transcends the Bible, what should our relationship with the second be in the light of the relationship we have with the first?

In this regard, we note that Heb 1:1–2 does not say that God has spoken through the texts of Scripture. It does not even say that God has spoken *through* the Scriptures, which reveal the Son! Instead, the text asserts simply that God has spoken through the *Son*. If we understand God's speaking to us through the Son as the fullness of God's word to us, then the word of God is not to be identified either exclusively or even principally with the Bible but rather with the Son. The Son *is* the word of God in its fullness; the word of God is ultimately personal and not literary.

Even a cursory look at the Scriptures would seem to confirm this thesis. To understand how the early Christians understood the relationship between word of God and Scripture, it would be expedient to turn our attention to some examples from the New Testament.

To start, there are passages that talk about how the Jews had nullified the word of God (*ton logon tou theou*) by their traditions (Matt 15:6; Mark 7:13). Clearly, such statements cannot refer to the documents of the scriptural texts, as if to say that the Jewish traditionalists had deleted or ignored the actual *words* of Scripture written on parchment. Nor is it sustainable that such a cancellation of the word of God had to do with their rejection of the *content* of the writing, because they were convinced that through their traditions, they were actually the defenders of the substance of Scriptures. In these examples, Jesus clearly understood the word of God as something that transcended the Scriptures such that the Jews were able to affirm the Scriptures with all their heart and at the same time completely deny the word of God.[26]

Turning our attention to Acts and the Epistles, "word of God," "word of the Lord," and simply "word" are used "mostly to denote the gospel, the message about God's work of salvation through the death and resurrection of Jesus Christ."[27] "Word of God" in these passages is to be considered as

26. It can be argued that the Jews denied the Scriptures in the sense of interpreting and/or applying them incorrectly. Surely, this was part of their denial. But this only helps to prove the thesis: the Bible that we can hold in our hands or put on a pedestal is not, *ontologically speaking*, identical to the word of God.

27. Fanning, "Word."

synonymous with the *kerygma*—"the word preached by the apostles and the early church as they went out as Spirit-empowered witnesses to Jesus."[28] Even in these New Testament writings, therefore, the word of God is not associated with the Bible per se.

In the most striking case of all, "word of God" refers to the eternal Son made flesh, the Logos, Jesus Christ, sent as the most excellent communication of the divine, "spoken" by God to creation concerning his person and will (John 1:1–2, 14). This passage takes us back to Heb 1:1–2, allowing us to fill out our theological interpretation of it even more. God exceeded his speaking through the prophets by speaking to us through the Son, because the latter is more excellent than the former. In the first chapter of his Gospel, John tells us that God's word is the communicative act of the Father whereby he manifests the Son in time and space, as a man. This final word of God encompasses not only the person of the incarnate Christ, but also his teachings and his works. On this view, the word of God in the fullest sense is clearly not reducible to the Bible; rather, it is to be understood as the perfect will of God manifested in and throughout the world definitively in his Son, born, dead, risen, and soon to return. Thus Jesus could rebuke the Jews for searching the Scriptures in hopes of finding eternal life without, however, coming to him so that they might live (John 5:39–40).

Even with this short and incomplete survey, we see that associating the word of God strictly with the Bible leads to a reductionist view of the first and an uneven view of the second.

THE INTELLECT, SPIRITUALITY, AND BIBLE FACTS

Despite the witness of Scripture itself that "word of God" has multifarious and equally important nuances (I have not even spoken of the word of God undergirding the whole of creation), mainline evangelicalism has tended to treat the concept as basically synonymous with the assertions of the Bible. One could argue that by emphasizing the distinction between "word of God" and "Bible" to the degree I have done here is to make a mountain of a molehill. The Bible is, after all, the primary source by which we come to know and evaluate the various connotations of "word of God." Moreover, there are biblical, theological, and historical precedents that indicate it is properly designated as such. What, then, is my concern?

28. Ibid.

To begin with, it is not semantic. In my view, to call the Bible the "word of God" is a practice that is neither undesirable nor wrong. The problem I am addressing is more subtle and therefore more perilous. It has to do with identifying word of God with the Bible in a *reductionistic* fashion. For this leads us into bibliolatry.

Above, I described bibliolatry as the belief that in order to know God spiritually—that is, to be reconciled to God in Christ and through the Spirit—it is *sufficient* to understand rightly what the Bible says and believe it. Admittedly, such a principle may appear harmless enough, especially for all who have grown up on the children's hymn "Jesus Loves Me." In our skeptical postmodern context, there is indeed something that rings refreshingly and undeniably true in the lyric: "Jesus loves me, this I know, for the Bible tells me so." On the other hand, were we to take such a statement as an absolute—as evangelicals often do—and follow it through to its logical and theological conclusion, it would place far too heavy a burden on the text to do what it is claimed to do, for it would ask human language not merely to contribute to a full knowledge of Christ's love, but basically to create it.

With even a modicum of reflection, we can begin to see how a mere knowledge of the Bible cannot create love for Christ in isolation from a personal, experiential work of God. A case may be made for this assertion. For example, hearing someone say aloud the text "I love you" may carry with it the deepest or the shallowest meaning and significance, depending on what we know of our collocutor apart from this statement. The dynamic would be the same were a third person to reveal by speech or writing that a friend had given up his life out of love to save ours. The actual *telling* of it—the message in and of itself—might create in one person a wholehearted devotion to the memory of that friend, while in another it might stir up mixed feelings or indifference, depending on the nature of the relationship the two shared. Regardless, none of these possible results could ever be the fruit of the message alone. There had to have been some sort of personal experience with the other along the way that allowed the words to have the resulting impact. Moreover, if such words were either directly or indirectly communicated to us concerning the actions of someone we hardly knew or perhaps had never even heard of (as is the case in many evangelistic encounters), the impact would be less powerful still, or even awkward and downright strange. According to this reasoning, reading or hearing the Bible's account of how Jesus loved us and died for us could not in and of itself be the efficient cause of a saving knowledge of and faith in him—though we must add that where it is totally missing, true Christian faith and devotion could hardly take place.

By reducing concepts such as "word of God" and "truth" to the statements of the Bible, evangelicals—either knowingly or unwittingly—have followed in the footsteps of the old Princeton scholastics (see chapter 1). These evangelical predecessors valiantly battled the onslaught of theological liberalism, scientific Darwinism, and philosophical materialism of the day, but in doing so adopted their adversaries' brimming optimism concerning the empirical method.[29] Consequently, their theology was grounded in observation and reason, reducing knowledge of God largely to what can be gleaned from a careful study of the facts presented in Scripture and diminishing faith to an intellectual and volitional assent to that content. It can be argued that even where the experiential dimension was given a place in the process of our coming to know God, it was nevertheless viewed in relation to its function within the more basic ratio-empirical model outlined above.[30]

Such an approach is to be avoided for at least two reasons. First, it presupposes a method of understanding that is too simplistic to account for the complex relationship known in contemporary hermeneutics as author-text-reader and its various ramifications.[31] This interpretive relationship is

29. As has already been noted in chapter 1, such optimism was never all-encompassing, insofar as even the most rationalist thinkers within the Princeton tradition advocated the necessary and primary role of the Holy Spirit in our interaction with the Bible. Nevertheless, the emphasis they placed on the empirical method has sometimes led to a practical marginalization of the Spirit for understanding Scripture. See below.

30. See, for example, Alexander, "Inaugural Discourse," 90. In discussing what it means to search the Scriptures, Alexander gives primacy of place theoretically to the work of the Holy Spirit, but in a telling methodological decision he places it "in the last place" of his discourse. Indeed, he seems to understand the Holy Spirit's work as subordinate to the scientific method, deepening and assisting the intellect's capacity to discover and comprehend.

31. Even though interpretive difficulties in the Bible have always been acknowledged throughout the history of the Judeo-Christian tradition, the findings of the last century in the fields of linguistics, literary theory, and philosophical and theological hermeneutics have caused contemporary interpreters more doubt than their predecessors concerning the possibility of making absolute claims based on reading Scripture. It is not that these disciplines have introduced doubt as to whether the Bible is trustworthy, but rather if any one interpretation of it can be taken as *absolute*. A positive result of this is an increased humility among interpreters that had previously been lacking within the greater Christian community. On the flipside and because of this, personal conviction of the truth—such as has always been a staple of Christian experience—is on the wane. What is needed in our contemporary situation is a way of reconciling the acknowledgement of

already complex enough when seeking to understand non-inspired texts. To bring to bear on it the weight of divine/human authorship, the doctrine of illumination, and the epistemological complications brought about by dealing with divine revelation on the one hand and the role of human faith on the other make the quaint lyrics of the children's song grossly insufficient as an explanation of how we come to know that God loves us through the Bible alone.

Second, this philosophy of interpretation easily leads to excessive or even primary dependence on our cognitive abilities, insofar as coming to (revealed) truth is narrowed down to deciphering the collected data in the right way with assistance from the Holy Spirit. Accordingly, the way to know God is not actually different from the method scientists use to know the material world—that is, by observation, deduction, and/or induction. All that is needed is confidence in our method of explicating the Scriptures and subsequent belief that our interpretation of them is true. It follows that the knowledge of God to be sought through Bible reading is not primarily of a personal nature but a cognitive one. Of course, it would be naïve to deny that there can be any encounter with God through Bible reading without engaging the mind in the Bible's propositional content. Hermeneutics is a spirally thing. The point is to avoid an approach that confuses the moment in which we come to an intellectual understanding of the biblical proposition with the fullness of communion with God. Therefore we also want to avoid the idea that coming to know God through the Bible is akin to doing a puzzle, which suggests we only encounter God once we have collected enough facts and put them in their proper places. Rather, the Scriptures serve us best when even in our most studious moments we are conversing with the living God, in the Spirit. Rather than being induced by God into a deeper relationship of love, however, the primary goal of doctrinalist Bible reading is the induction of knowledge of God from the empirically-funded collection of accumulated biblical facts.

Once again, the problem is not the method per se; rather it lies in reducing the question of Christian truth and spirituality to the method. Such a reduction inevitably leads to a rationalist or objectivist faith that ultimately asserts that knowledge of God is obtained primarily through the intellect working correctly on the clear revelatory statements of the Bible.

---

the complex and subtle nature of (biblical) hermeneutics on the one hand with a robust, sure-footed historical faith that is able and willing to identify heresy and error. For a critique of the kind of method practiced by Princeton as being hermeneutically naïve, see Dulles, *Models of Revelation*, 49.

DOCTRINE AND EXPERIENCE

Of course, to warn against an overly rational approach to the Bible does not warrant erring in the opposite extreme—that is, outright rejecting the claim that we may and do know God through the mind by normal human reasoning. We are to love God with our entire being, including the mind. Among other things, this surely indicates divine approval of a meticulous examination of the Scriptures using the intellectual faculties God has given us, for reason is a God-given faculty for attaining spiritual knowledge of the divine.[32]

Indeed, a hearty application of our intellects to Scripture is sorely needed in many evangelical contexts, but only as long as it is practiced within an environment of daily, embodied, cross-centered spirituality. This is to say, it is the sovereign, active indwelling Holy Spirit, forming Christ in the body and lives of those who are daily dying to themselves, that creates a spiritual milieu suitable for knowing God through rational and empirical methods. It is in this way that we are to understand the primacy of the Holy Spirit over our reason in coming to know God even in intellectual endeavors. In biblical faith, there is never any indication that the believer must consciously oppress his or her reason, in order to "channel" the Spirit that resides within. Nor is it ever suggested that the seeker of God must "empty" his or her mind to know God. Such practices suggest a kind of mysticism that biblical spirituality resolutely rejects.

In the New Testament, we find quite a different type of relationship between the intellect and spirituality. Rather than being a question of minimizing or oppressing rational activity, the knowledge of God depends on an active or conscious *submission* of our intellects to the Spirit. As Paul understood it, the mind of the disciple is to be neither limited or eliminated but rather filled and directed by the Spirit so that every thought might be taken captive to Christ (2 Cor 10:5). A humble rather than nimble mind is therefore of primary importance when it comes to reaping the harvest of the biblical statements. As Martin Luther put it, the cross is the one indispensible experience basic to doing genuine Christian theology: "It is living, dying, and even being condemned which makes a theologian—not

---

32. It is certainly the case that all the various academic fields in biblical studies have true value in the process of knowing God as he has revealed himself. This would include, for example, such disciplines as archeology and textual criticism, which are strongly data-based (though they certainly are not void of an interpretative aspect). These disciplines are useful even when performed by aggressively anti-Christian people, because facts do assist in the pursuit of knowledge and truth.

Bibliolatry

reading, speculating and understanding."[33] Indeed, many great minds have gone astray in their doctrine and life not because of "too much" intellect but because of a proud mind that knew little or nothing experientially of the work of the cross. For this reason, the Holy Spirit was impeded from revealing Christ to and in them. In other words, they did not perform their interpretation of the Bible within a context of a daily, cross-bearing, embodied spirituality.

While there is definitely a need in the church for the kind of detailed exegesis often associated with a scientific study of the text, it must not and cannot reign supreme as a way of Bible reading if the gospel is to remain relevant either for the world at large or for the church. Furthermore, to my mind, even a "scientific reading" of the Bible that seeks to be exegetically thorough with the text should never be devoid of a healthy pietist principle undergirding its interpretation.

What I have in mind here is something akin to the exhortation of the fifteenth-century ascetic Thomas à Kempis to the "religious" of his day. He wrote that the reader of Scripture, on the one hand, should be careful to read each part of Holy Writ in the spirit in which it was written. This amounts to a plea for an interpretation that avoids abstraction of the text from its context. The goal of this principle, however, is to seek profit for the soul rather than eloquence of exposition. Furthermore, à Kempis urged that in reading the Scriptures, intellectual curiosity should be limited, lest we be seduced by understanding and end up mulling over what ought simply be read and passed by.[34] Less is more.

While this approach might appear impractical for certain kinds of assignments, its attractiveness lies in the fact that it points to a submission of method and mind to the "whim" of the Spirit without eliminating either. Neither reason, observation, nor learned investigation are dismissed out of hand from Bible reading, though curiosity for curiosity's sake is signaled out as vanity, an unfit mind-set for rightly handling the word of God. Rather than inquisitiveness, the Spirit of God should be allowed to point us to what is most important in the text. The idea is to have the risen Lord speaking to us through our particular method of reading the text—illuminating, guiding, and even censoring.

Such an approach does not advocate that all Bible reading should be personal meditation, for that too would be an unnecessary reduction.

---

33. Cited in McGrath, "Theology and Experience," 68.
34. Kempis, *Imitation of Christ*, 1.5.

However, it does suggest that even when studying Scripture for, let's say, writing commentaries, we should seek to avoid addressing the text simply as if it were an archeological site full of interesting artifacts to uncover. There is a sense in which it is also that. Nevertheless, even in a rigorous scholarly endeavor, the goal is to discern what the Spirit of God would have us concentrate on for the particular task we have been called to do. After all, not even writing top-level commentary transcends the vocation of the Holy Spirit. By working in this way, perhaps our commentaries might come to benefit the church as much as they do the academy by bearing the fruit of gifted exegetes searching out the real-time mind of Christ rather than merely the bare historical facts contained within the text.[35] Facts are important, of course, but only relative to context; the Spirit leads into all truth.[36]

Taking this approach, the Bible need not be perceived as a field of research in which God-facts are at the interpreter's beck and call to be exhumed and examined. Rather, it can be understood as a meeting place to which the Holy Spirit leads the disciple to listen to and speak with the risen Lord. In this kind of reading, opening the Scriptures is similar to entering into an elaborate English garden in which the reader, guided by the landscape architect, comes to see this and then that corner of perfection and beauty as directed by the only one who really knows the complete layout. Furthermore, the Spirit does not lead in such a way as to dispense "truth in a vacuum" but rather to marry it to the reader's current spiritual state or walk, which is itself representative of what God is doing in the church. In this way, personal giftedness and rigorous Bible study come together for the building up of the body of Christ. The whole of Scripture is expounded, but not abstractly, as if for some assumed, timeless, universal readership.

The significance of such an approach to Scripture is evident. By definition, divine revelation is always and only manifested for the purposes

---

35. In any case, contemporary hermeneutic theory has shown us that even the most objective commentators can never be completely free from picking and choosing according to some sort of agenda, whether conscious or unknown. In other words, objectivity always comes with an asterisk.

36. This kind of approach aligns with the best of the Reformed thinkers. For example, in commenting on John Calvin's view of reading the Scriptures, Timothy George writes, "The study of the Bible was meant to be transformative at the most basic level of the human person, leading to communion with God. The spiritual power of the Bible emerges for Christians from the fact that the 'Word of God' is not just a matter of words. Jesus Christ is the substantial Word, the eternal Logos who was made flesh—*verbum incarnatum*—for us and for our salvation" (George, "Reading the Bible with the Reformers," 27–28).

God has decreed it to have for the instruction, admonition, exhortation, and the building up in Christ of human beings. There is no sense in which Scripture ever understands itself as truth in the abstract; it is always *truth for someone*. Of course, God exists independently of the creature, and in this sense, so does truth. But *revealed* truth, such as the Bible claims to be, is geared towards the instruction in salvation of *people*. The attempt to grasp truth as it relates to God, in all his inaccessible light, is the height of presumption, but it is also presumptuous to attempt to extract truth from Scripture's revealedness in order to make it into a pristine fact of divinity. Alister McGrath makes a similar point, stressing that the intellectual pursuit of reflecting theologically on revealed truth must never be removed from revelation's goal of bringing the whole person into a transformative encounter with Christ:

> Christian theology cannot remain faithful to its subject matter if it regards itself as purely propositional or cognitive in nature. The Christian encounter with God is transformative. As Calvin pointed out, to know God is to be changed by God; true knowledge of God leads to worship, as the believer is caught up in a transforming and renewing encounter with the living God. To know God is to be changed by God. As Søren Kierkegaard pointed out in his *Unscientific Postscript*, to know the truth is to be known by the truth. "Truth" is something which affects our inner being, as we become involved in "an appropriation process of the most passionate inwardness."[37]

We admit that molecules, monkeys, and Mussolini are facts that exist in natural history independently of how we experience them. But these are not special, divine revelations. They can be abstracted by the natural mind because they are natural. The application of natural reason alone to knowing that which comes from heaven, however, must of necessity be reductionistic, even by natural reason's own logic. The Spirit who came from heaven must reveal revelation through encounter if it is to be relevant; *living* knowledge of God can never be obtained without illumination.[38] Thus, bare natural reason outside the proper spiritual context can never know God,

---

37. McGrath, "Theology and Experience," 67.

38. Illumination on this account would not necessarily be a series of individual "enlightenments" of how the facts fit together but a context of encounter. The intellect remains hard at work in making sense of the biblical material, but only as it is embedded within an environment of daily, embodied, cross-bearing spirituality so that it is sensitive to the guiding of the Spirit.

even if it has comprehended the facts of God to near perfection. To know divine things purely through natural means is not to know them spiritually, as God intends them to be known.

BIBLIOLATRY AND THE SPIRITUALITY OF THE BIBLE

This discussion logically provokes an important question: Is the Bible by and of itself something spiritual, or do the Scriptures *become* spiritual only when they lead the reader to an encounter with the risen Christ? The answer to this very neo-orthodox question, I would maintain, is both.

The Scriptures are inherently spiritual, for they have their origin in the Spirit of God (Rom 7:14). Nevertheless, the spirituality of the Bible is not completely inherent to the text, for the sole function of the inspired Scripture is to point *human beings* towards a spiritual life in Christ. To put it bluntly, a spiritual Bible without a readership serves no purpose. If God had revealed his word in writing to be a monument to truth in isolation from its readers and hearers, then we could make a case that its spirituality derives from itself alone. However, the divinely stated goal of the Scriptures is to instruct, exhort, rebuke, and encourage human beings in Christ. From this perspective, therefore, it is legitimate to tie the question of the spirituality of the Bible to its readers as well. Once we allow for this, however, we still need to address the observable fact that the spirituality of the Bible is not transferred automatically to anyone who reads it. Indeed, we can learn the whole of Scripture by heart without having a spiritual knowledge of it. Why is that? The answer is for the same reason that the law, though being "life," can "bring death to me" if I am carnally-minded—that is, if I am blinded and seduced by the deceptive influences of sin (Rom 7:13–14).

The principle of interpretation I am advocating is not something new; indeed, it was received from the earliest days of the church, as is verified both in Paul's assertion that only the spiritually-minded can receive the things of God (1 Cor 2:10–16) and by Augustine in the fifth century, who sustained that in order to understand the things of God, we must believe—*crede, ut intelligas*—and not vice versa.[39] Whatever else Paul and Augustine

---

39. Augustine, *Sermons* 43.7, 9 cited in Becker, *Fundamental Theology*, 70n14. It must be noted that the full Latin formula often shortened to *crede, ut intelligas* in Augustine's sermon is *Intellige ut credas meum verbum; crede ut intelligas verbum Dei*, which translated is "understand my word, in order to believe; believe the word of God in order to understand" (ibid.). It is, therefore, clear that Augustine was no fideist, for believing was to think with assent (Augustine, *Treatise on the Predestination of the Saints*, 5) upon the

may have intended with their statements, they certainly wanted to underline that in some fundamental way the spiritual (i.e., Spirit-mindedness, fellowship with God, faith) is indispensable to proper or true knowledge of the things of God.

With the a priori exclusion of any "spiritual rule" of biblical interpretation, bibliolatry ultimately understands the intellect not only as the repository of the knowledge of God, but also its efficient cause. It does so notwithstanding adherence to the Reformation doctrine of the internal witness of the Spirit. How so? By giving disproportionate priority to another of the Reformers doctrines—Scripture as its own interpreter. In practice, bibliolaters give so much attention to this principle that the internal witness of the Spirit becomes almost a figurehead doctrine: all that is necessary for a true knowledge of God is a sound intellect employing good exegetical method applied to a self-explanatory Bible.

In the final analysis, bibliolatry reduces the word of God to the Bible and the Bible to the biblical data contained therein. Moreover, it exalts sound method to a place reserved by the Bible itself for the Holy Spirit as the efficient causal agent of our knowledge of God. In this way, as seen above, doctrinalism reduces the Holy Spirit to a mere helpmate to our intellectual efforts in understanding what the Bible has to say. In still other words, it effectively reverses the roles, so that we wind up honoring the creature above the Creator. Once again, this is idolatry.

In modern traditionalist evangelicalism, Bible study has generally been set over and against an experiential approach to knowing God. In this, we can identify a reason for the dissatisfaction of many traditional evangelical believers who display an abundance of intellectual integrity but often lament a lack of spiritual vitality in their lives and communities. All this is normal when we conflate a book about a person with the person himself. Such an approach, when applied to knowing Christ, is destined to produce a rationalist, traditionalist, and ultimately weary faith.

What *is* the Bible essentially, that bibliolaters should make this move? It is a grammatically-based means by which a living Christ is presented to us by God's Spirit in human language. I do not emphasize this in order to minimize the value of the written word but simply to describe it. The "grammar" of the word of God is of fundamental importance to the Christian

---

Scriptures. Nevertheless, Augustine did stress "the mutual interaction of faith and understanding in the interpretation of the Scriptures for the sake of true knowledge of God" (Becker, *Fundamental Theology*, 71).

DOCTRINE AND EXPERIENCE

faith because God is by nature a communicator. Insofar as he has chosen to communicate to human beings through human language, the Bible has a central and fundamental role to play in knowing God. Furthermore, as stated by the Reformers, God dwells in the reading and exposition of Scripture by means of the Holy Spirit. For this reason, we reject any attempt either explicitly or implicitly to minimize the importance of the Scriptures and the ongoing and thorough study of them in the church. Similarly, we flatly refuse the insidious teaching so common in our time that the Spirit brings life but that too much Bible knowledge brings death.[40]

Nevertheless, the warning stands: we must be careful not to give sole primacy to a book, even if it is from heaven. In a certain sense this is difficult to write, for the Bible as gift of God is and should be dear to the heart of every regenerate believer. Nevertheless, it is still only an endowment. Every good gift has come down from heaven, but this does not mean we should venerate the gift—that is, unless it is the word of God in the flesh! The Bible is God's word, but it does not exhaust all that the word of God is. As we saw above, to know the Bible is not the same as knowing God, and therefore it is not sufficient in itself as a collection of documents to communicate the whole of what knowing God is for us. When Jesus says that he himself is the truth, the way, and the life (John 14:6), he challenges and even defies all propositionalist epistemologies that would enclose truth completely within written or spoken statements. In the final analysis, humanity needs to experience Jesus, not propositions that reveal him—though admittedly without those propositions, no one can come to know him as he wants to be known.

"Word of God" ultimately refers to the person of the Son, who is the decisive communication of God to us (John 1:18; 14: 7–9; Heb 1:1–4). To conflate the propositional word with the personal one is a misstep, for ontologically the former is infinitely inferior to the latter. Such a fusion can only serve to distance us from a personal, daily, encountering relationship with God and ground us in a formal one, robbing the Christian life of its full vitality and power. Such an "exchange" is easier to make than we might imagine.

---

40. This opposition is usually grounded in a wrong-headed interpretation of 2 Cor 3:6.

BIBLIOLATRY, *SOLA SCRIPTURA*, AND THE LORDSHIP OF THE HOLY SPIRIT

The doctrinalist understanding of *sola scriptura* has in many cases transmuted into a mere construct of the Reformation principle. For the Reformers, it meant that the Bible is the supreme authority in all matters of doctrine and practice "in opposition to Roman Catholic claims on behalf of tradition, merit, Mary and the saints."[41] The Reformers originally understood the authority of the Bible in terms of "a conflict between competing authorities." As such, it is rooted in polemics.[42] Abstracted from its historical context, however, *sola scriptura* has often become a mantra for a Christian postivist *epistemology*. In this form, it no longer merely contests extra-biblical authorities, but also non-empirical methods of knowing. Nowhere is this more evident than in bibliolatry's protest against the possibility of knowing God today through the direct and personal guidance of the Holy Spirit. This, in turn, brings up the question of what the lordship of the Holy Spirit means for the bibliolater.

Bibliolaters (though not all doctrinalists) axiomatically rule out the possibility that Christ today communicates to his people directly through the Holy Spirit. For these evangelicals, to make a claim of direct communication is tantamount to negating the doctrine of *sola scriptura*.[43] The reason for this is an epistemology that opposes any way of coming to true knowledge of God apart from empirical Bible investigation.[44] This epistemological foundation is what gives legs to scholastic fundamentalism wherever it manifests itself.

Adhering to this philosophy of knowledge, bibliolatry risks replacing faithfulness to the risen Christ with obedience to an ethical code or dogma. By making the printed page the sole source of divine guidance, bibliolaters circumvent the possibility of the Spirit's full, effective lordship, because it shuts the Spirit up by shutting the Spirit in within the sphere of Bible exposition. (I shall return to this theme). This is the spiritual result of doctrinalism's inadequate view of the word of God. Amongst bibliolaters, there is of course much talk about a personal kinship with the Spirit, but

---

41. Cole, "Sola Scriptura," 21.
42. Ibid.
43. See, for example, Silva, "Henry Blackaby's Mysticism-Lite."
44. R. C. Sproul reminds us that for Luther and the Reformers, the Bible was not the sole authoritative source in the church but rather the only *infallible* one (Sproul, "Sola Scriptura," 104).

the main relationship is really with the Bible. In doctrinalist spirituality, one often hears "It is written." This is most welcome, but almost completely missing from their vocabulary is the "Spirit said to me" language of Acts. Indeed, one prominent critic of neo-pietism puts such talk in the disapproving category of "extrabiblical 'words from the Lord.'"[45] Such language is frowned upon as apparently unbiblical, though it is found in the Bible, I would argue, *paradigmatically*.[46]

Of course, bibliolaters do not claim that the Holy Spirit has ceased leading the church; they do claim, however, that he guides in only one way—through illuminating the truth of Scripture to our hearts and minds.[47] This would not be so objectionable were it not the case that what bibliolaters usually mean by this is that the Spirit only speaks when the Bible is actually opened in reading, studying, preaching, or recalling. They seem not to take into consideration that Scripture-infused, Spirit-filled, faithful Christians have the mind of Christ, which makes them, in a matter of speaking, "walking Bibles." Surely, the Spirit of God can still guide people in revealing his specific will, as he did with Abraham, Moses, Samuel, Elijah, Jesus, and the apostles. This is not to say that in speaking thus God intends to add new doctrine and practice to the once-and-for-all delivered gospel. On the other hand, the Scriptures themselves never show God restricting his direct communication to his people to the standards of orthodox Christian doctrine. Indeed, a number of the examples of God speaking to people in Scripture is decisively *situational* in character, having nothing to do directly with normative doctrine or practice.

Two popular arguments bibliolaters put forth as evidence for their view are weak at best. The first is the "canonical argument." It states that since the last canonical book was written towards the end of the first century (or was it since the establishment of the canon in the third and fourth centuries?) the Holy Spirit has stopped speaking in a direct way to believers and now only speaks through the written word. For this reason, there is no

---

45. MacArthur, "False Prophets and Lying Wonders."

46. As chapter 3 will make clear, I do not believe all of Acts is to be taken as paradigmatic for the church. The deeply personal relationship of the early disciples with the Spirit as Lord, however, was promised by Jesus himself once the Comforter would come. Furthermore, while one can cogently argue from the latter epistles that there was a shift away from what I believe are the non-paradigmatic performances of signs and wonders by the apostles, there is no evidence that leads us to conclude that the Spirit stopped guiding the church by speaking, telling, testifying, forbidding, allowing, etc.

47. MacArthur, "False Prophets and Lying Wonders."

longer need for him to speak to us any other way, especially not directly to our spirits. However, this is a theological supposition, not an argument. Indeed, we are hard-pressed to locate the source from which this authoritative claim derives, as neither the Bible nor the church has ever made it dogma. We are left wondering if it was an extra-biblical revelation of the Holy Spirit given directly to certain evangelicals!

The second argument is even less convincing. We might call it the "guesswork argument." It goes like this: The Spirit cannot still be talking to us directly, because how can we ever really know if it is the voice of the Lord or our own thoughts, ideas, desires, or even the devil speaking? To this point, we might ask how the biblical prophets knew it was the Lord speaking to them. Did they receive a divinely enhanced, paranormal extra sense—totally lacking in post-apostolic Christianity—that enabled them to distinguish God's speaking from their own thoughts? Or has God simply created human beings with the ability to discern his voice under the right conditions? This would appear to be the case, as the prophets themselves seemed to come to a recognition of the Lord's speech through most ordinary human methods, including repetition, experience, listening to counsel, and trial and error (e.g., 1 Sam 3:1–11). That this mundane human capacity was sufficient for the prophets is discernable in that after pronouncing, "Thus says the Lord," we have no scriptural evidence that the prophets were overly anxious to see if their prophecy would come to pass. They of course knew that the penalty for false prophecy was death, but they were somehow assured that it was the Lord and not Satan or their own imaginations speaking to them. The same can be said of Peter and Paul. How did Peter know it was the Lord and not the hot sun causing hallucinations on the rooftop? How did Paul know it was the risen Lord on the road to Damascus and not some manical, guilt-driven figment of his imagination caused by his intense hatred for the "charlatan" Jesus of Nazareth? Both Peter and Paul seemed to recognize God without any *special* enabling from the Spirit. Finally, if the devil's direct speech can beguile our minds, cannot the Lord at least keep pace with his adversary and convince us of the truth of his will when desiring to speak to his own in this way?

To claim direct guidance is not at all to say that the Holy Spirit today reveals new truths concerning doctrine or practice. It is to say, however, that the Spirit of Christ guides faithful men and women in their day-to-day walk with him. Why this is so odious to bibliolaters is difficult to understand outside an adherence to deeply rooted positivist epistemology's assertion that legitimate truth claims can only be made on the basis of "facts" derived from the scientific method.

Of course, there are going to be both charlatans as well as sincere but deceived "hearers" of God who mistake other voices for that of the Lord. But are there not also false Bible expositors who twist the written word around until it is fleshly and diabolical, not to mention sincere Bible interpreters who fall into error because of their determination to make the text fit their assumptions? Should we argue that the Spirit no longer speaks through the Bible because it can be interpreted subjectively or "heard" erroneously?[48]

This brings up the question as to what is the essential difference between the Holy Spirit revealing God's situational will for me through a Bible reading in my study and the Spirit speaking in a personal time of reflection as I walk in the garden or kneel before the throne. Of course, the more Scripture permeates my mind, the better I will be able to discern the Spirit's guidance through other channels. Nevertheless, one also needs to consider the stories of many believers who have been called in areas of the world where the Bible is not available. Somehow God gets through to them just the same—at least initially—in dreams, visions, or by other means.

The Bible is God's sure word. It is the only normative authority for the church in all matters of doctrine and practice. No individual's experience of God is *ipso facto* binding on anyone—at least not in the same sense as the Bible is. Yet important distinctions need to be made concerning God's situational guidance. First, what does it mean in terms of guidance that the Bible is infallibly authoritative for the Christian? Does it mean that whenever we blindly point to a passage in the open Bible, the precise passage on which our finger lands is God's specific will for us at that point in our lives? Does the Bible authorize me to go to the grieving mother in my congregation and tell her she has to stop mourning her dead child and celebrate God's goodness, because when turning to Scripture to console her my eye fell upon the exhortation to rejoice always in the Lord (Phil 4:4)? Perhaps, but perhaps not! Bibliolaters are sometimes known to think and act in just this fashion, simply because "It is written." Not only are they often insensitive to the discerning lordship of the Holy Spirit, they don't

---

48. By "subjective" I mean knowledge claims based on personal feelings, opinions, prejudices, desires, and the like. A more philosophical definition for the term would refer to how we experience things in our own mind. In the latter case, one cannot help but be subjective even during the most scientifically sound examination of the Bible, for the very act of performing the study is itself an experience that has to be related to by the subject.

always consider other passages of Scripture that would lead them to act more appropriately (e.g., Rom 12:15). Second, we have to admit that were the Holy Spirit to speak on the Father's behalf to an individual or a church apart from (though not in conflict with) the Bible, this word would be no less binding than the Scripture *for that particular situation*. For it is the same Holy Spirit who inspired the Scriptures and who speaks personally to God's people. One is reminded of the church of Antioch's revelation in prayer and fasting to send Paul and Barnabas as missionaries. Would not the refusal to send them have been as direct an act of disobedience to God as refusing the written command not to steal (Eph 4:28; cf. Exod 20:15)? Or if Paul, Silas, and Timothy had forced their way to preach the gospel in Asia after the Spirit had "forbidden" it, would they not have been just as disobedient as if they had coveted their neighbor's wife (Acts 16:6–7; cf. Exod 20:17)? What if Paul had disregarded the dream that directed him to Macedonia or Peter had ignored the vision that led him to the house of Cornelius? Would they not have been held accountable for their disobedience to the word of God communicated to them? Of course, if God only speaks through the Scriptures, then all these points are moot, but then we would have to deal with a Bible that gives such examples while at the same time denying their continuing reality. On the other hand, if God still communicates personally to his people through sermons, prayer, fasting, reflection, fellowship, worship, dreams, and visions, then when he does speak, it is clearly no less binding, just as it is no less God who is speaking.

This last point brings another important distinction to the fore. While Christians no longer require new knowledge concerning doctrine and practice, they still need the Holy Spirit's guidance so that they might (a) understand Scripture rightly, (b) understand the particulars of their lives in light of the Scriptures, (c) apply Scripture to life both generally and particularly, and (d) discern the will of God for situations not specifically addressed in the Bible. (I return to this last point below).

Doctrinalists in general are wary of talk about extra-biblical guidance of the Spirit, though not completely without good reason. There is some risk in teaching that the Holy Spirit is the living Lord (2 Cor 3:17–18), and many abuses do in fact ensue (see chapter 3). It is apparently safer to restrict the Spirit's "speaking" to the illumination of the inspired Scriptures, because when we are not sure if it is really the Spirit revealing, there is a seemingly objective fallback measure—namely, proper exegetical methods applied to the text. But there is also great risk in making the Bible the only arena in which the Spirit speaks. Perhaps the main danger is that this approach tends to make daily obedience to God a question of adherence to a set of prescriptions rather than to a living Person. After all, God's commandments are God's and not the Bible's in a strict sense. God is a living, personal being, whereas the Bible is a library composed of documents. To conflate the two invariably leads to a sort of legalism, which we may define in the evangelical doctrinalist context as a devotion to God that can be obtained only through the letter of the written word. The Jewish religious leaders were guilty of doing just this and, as a result, failed to recognize God staring them in the face (John 5:39–40). In a fully-orbed Christian faith, legalism is prevented by the lordship of the Holy Spirit, who continuously brings us back to the person of Christ so that our obedience might derive from a personal loving relationship with God and not merely a strict adherence to a set of laws and prescriptions.

In an attempt to purify the church from pietist and experientialist influences, it is not unheard of for bibliolaters to lump moderate charismatics (e.g., Wayne Grudem) and conservative Baptists (e.g., Henry Blackaby) together with excessive charismatics such as Benny Hinn.[49] A particular target group for bibliolaters is the so-called Spiritual Formation Movement, which is experiential without necessarily being experientialist.[50] The typical condemnation of the spiritual formation movement is that it has abandoned *sola scriptura*, harking back instead to a legalistic mystic spirituality with rules and practices aimed at helping us draw closer to God experientially. Doctrinalist critics are fearful that this kind of spirituality both evolves from and inevitably devolves back into a works-righteousness mystic mentality.[51] The irony in this is that bibliolaters are arguably more

---

49. MacArthur, "False Prophets and Lying Wonders."

50. Some well-known contemporary names associated with this movement are Dallas Willard, Richard Forster, John Ortberg, Larry Crabb, Henri Nouwen, and Eugene Peterson. Precursors to the movement range from Thomas à Kempis and Ignatius of Loyola to C. S. Lewis, Oswald Chambers, and Dietrich Bonhoeffer. One could perhaps cite people like Phillip Yancey, Tim Keller, and John Piper as sympathizers, especially concerning the question of what prayer consists of. NB: Piper's high regard for and reliance on Martyn Lloyd-Jones clearly puts him in the experientialist camp for some bibliolaters, e.g., Bowers, "False Teachings."

51. This may happen, but it is not an inherent outcome of a spirituality that values spiritual disciplines. This is certainly the case for conservative evangelical such as Dallas Willard, Donald Whitney, and Henry Blackaby who are grace-centered and Bible-centered in the best of the evangelical tradition. But it is also true even for Catholic mystics who, like Thomas à Kempis and Ignatius of Loyola, stressed that the spiritual exercises

susceptible to works-righteousness than those they criticize, albeit in a different way than how they conceive it with regards to the Spiritual Formation Movement.

Evangelical blogger and author Frank Viola makes this very point when he identifies an insidious legalism within (Reformed) evangelicalism that goes deeper than attempts to earn salvation through human works. It is manifested in an understanding of *sanctification* as coming from the believer's own efforts at trying to be a "good Christian." These evangelical legalists, Viola blogs, are identifiable by certain modes of behavior. They "tend to push their own personal standards onto everyone else . . . are quick to judge other people's motives, thinking the worst of them and their intentions . . . confuse obedience with trying to serve God in their own strength . . . demand other people do things that they themselves would never carry out . . . regard the sins of others as more severe and grievous than their own."[52] This evangelical legalism, I would submit, comes about in part from a misunderstanding of how to employ the Bible in the believer's daily obedience to God.

From a certain perspective, the bibliolatry credo could be *sola scriptura/non Spiritus Sanctus*. Obedience is to an ethical code severed from the experiential lordship of the Holy Spirit: "I am walking in right fellowship with God only to the degree that I am submitted to all that the Bible says." Surely, this approach can only be fruitful up to a point. Yet it is common to find doctrinalists insisting all that is needed to answer life's thorniest questions—all that is required to understand and do God's will for any situation—is to defer to the Bible.

What doctrinalists appear unwilling to accept is that the Bible on its own simply cannot (nor is designed to) account for all the particulars of life in Christ. It does not and cannot address the infinite number of perplexing combinations that arise in the ebb and flow of daily human living, not to mention in the course of serious Christian discipleship. Of course, the Bible contains all the general principles we need, but as experience teaches us, rarely is there a shortage of intricate life-situations that cause us to scratch our heads and ask what God's will is for us *in this particular circumstance*. Should we speak up or be quiet? Should we encourage or

---

were not to be practiced in order to gain merit with God but rather were enabled only by God's grace to help discipline the body, mind, and soul to be more centered on Christ's work and person. For a sampling of such unwarranted criticism, see Gilley, "Contemplative Prayer"; Silva, "Henry Blackaby's Mysticism-Lite."

52. Viola, "Legalism, License, Lordship and Liberty."

DOCTRINE AND EXPERIENCE

rebuke? Should we preach or pray, act or wait? Often we find no solace investigating the Bible because we find all the various alternatives taught and practiced therein at differing moments. Ironically, these are by no means contradictions, insofar as they are simply either general principles to be applied accordingly or the written account of how the Spirit of God guided the biblical characters in this or that particular situation. To pit the Spirit's personal guidance against the Scriptures, as doctrinalists tend to do, is, in a very profound way, unbiblical.

That we need direct personal guidance from God at times in no way diminishes the Bible; in fact, it can be argued that this enhances it by bringing together God's word through the Scripture and God's word through the Spirit in perfect, dynamic harmony. Doctrinalists rightly point out that it is condemnable to substitute personal revelation for Scripture. The Bible *is* our measure for all truth. But this fact does not in any way rule out that God can also guide personally, situationally, directly, and according to truth; it only means that what the Spirit genuinely speaks will invariably line up with what the Bible says in one way or another.

Bibliolaters fail to see that an approach to Christian obedience that relies on the Bible but not on the situational guidance of the Spirit cannot help but adhere to an abstracted ethical code. The phenomena appear to bear this out, for though each particular Christian culture develops its own particular ethics of obedience (usually depending on preferred biblical doctrines), they nonetheless all seem to produce the same general kind of fruit: dogmatic, insensitive, easy answers to life's complicated problems. Unbelievers often walk away from bibliolatrous counsel asking themselves where the mercy and compassion of Christ is to be found. Believers wind up either crushed, angered, confused, or slavishly convinced and puffed up by such guidance.

Theologically, the problem stems from the misguided belief that the operation of the Holy Spirit is somehow restricted to revealing the propositional truths of Scripture to us. Once these truths have been comprehend, the intellect and common sense take over in applying the biblical data to the details of each individual problem. In a certain sense, this model proposes that God has been out of the picture for two thousand years. According to this view, God effectively guided ancient Israel and the first-century church, but he does not guide us today in the same way. Rather, it is up to the church to learn how the Lord guided his people twenty centuries ago so it can make applications today. Guidance from above has been taken captive by application from below. The Holy Spirit was once Lord of all but is so no longer; now, he simply assists our minds in extracting principles from the historical writings of a people for whom he really had been Lord.

According to a biblical spirituality, however, the Holy Spirit does not merely illumine the mind to Scripture, but also guides us directly by speaking in any number of ways to lead us to understand and care for the problem at hand. The Spirit illuminates the mind to relevant Scripture, but also to the specific details of the particular case. In this way, we are "walked through" the crisis by the sure counsel of the risen Christ, who is by our side. The Spirit's real-time guidance is essential for the church. Christ knew what was in people's hearts and could read the signs to identify the essential obstacles to a godly resolution. We need to learn directly *from* him and not only *about* him in this regard. Just as the Twelve walked and talked with the Master, so too can modern-day disciples, for he is risen and is in us.

Christ's penetrating perception of the people and problems he encountered was not the result of his special abilities as God incarnate or of his thorough knowledge of the Law. It was rather the fruit of his communion with the Father through the Holy Spirit. He spoke and worked only as he heard and observed the Father speaking and working. His wisdom and intelligence came from heaven through the Spirit as well as from his study of the Law, the Psalms, and the Prophets. Christ's spirituality, therefore, was rooted just as much in the regular guidance of the Spirit, with whom he lived in the closest intimacy, as in his illumined understanding of Scripture. Only in this way was Jesus able to be scriptural in all he said and did without being legalistic. Like Christ, we are not to do anything other than what we hear the Father and the Son *speak*. How do we know what they are speaking? They speak it to us through God's written word and through his Spirit as we walk in loving obedience to his commandments.

The kind of obedience that arises from a determined will to depend slavishly on the commandments apart from dependence on the personal lordship of the Spirit inevitably leads to legalism of some form. On the other hand, obedience first and foremost to the person of Christ through the Spirit will ensure that we handle Scripture correctly and help us avoid the suffocating trap of a spirituality deriving from an abstract ethical code that ultimately leads us to bow down to the great rationalist gods: Respectability and Uniformity.

DOCTRINE AND EXPERIENCE

CONCLUDING THOUGHTS

Summing up, on the one hand we have the revelation of the Son. In a certain moment in history, the word became flesh, died on the cross, rose from the dead, and returned to the Father in glory. On the other, we have inspired commentary on this historical revelation as the written witness of God's work in saving humankind. The Bible is therefore the revelation of God because it reveals Christ with spiritual words as God revealed him (1 Cor 2:13). However, neither the power nor the authority of the written revelation resides in some inherent quality in the words themselves. If this were the case, anyone who had ever read a page of the Bible would have encountered the living God spiritually and been born from above. On the other hand, faith only comes by hearing (or reading) in human language the gospel of Jesus Christ, understanding it, and assenting to it in faith.

From this vantage point, we can claim that the scientific approach to the Bible—the application of our natural intellectual faculties to the tangible biblical documents—is essential for a genuine Christian spirituality, insofar as it creates an intellectually lucid environment in which the Holy Spirit can point us beyond the human qualities of the words to the divine realities being described. (Plato lives!) However, it is also true that one can read the Bible, understand its doctrinal content correctly, and even assent to it without ever grasping heaven. If the Son does not speak to us *through* the written word, the grammar of the Bible alone is not capable of producing life. In this sense, Barth was right. The Bible becomes the word of God only when we meet Christ in it.

In this, Barth finds an unlikely ally in the renowned evangelical preacher, writer, and thinker A. W. Tozer.[53] In a sermon on human consciousness, Tozer wrote approvingly of a preacher he once heard in New York City. The

---

53. NB: I do not want to lump Barth and Tozer more closely together than they actually were. Tozer's views derived from a pietist emphasis on the inner life. To read the Bible without Christ illuminating the mind and finally applying the words to our hearts is an exercise in futility. Barth, on the other hand, was known for his anti-pietist sentiments. Rather, he comes to his conclusions on the basis of a dialectical theology, stressing the insufficiency of human words to connect us to the utterly transcendent God. Thus, if the Bible is to be effective Godwards, it is necessary to encounter the risen Christ there. Notwithstanding their starting points, however, both Barth and Tozer were concerned with showing that the Bible, as an entity in itself, was insufficient to connect us to God. Both also understood the Bible as a God-given means to a genuine spirituality (i.e., God-connectedness) by facilitating an existential meeting with the living Christ through human words.

subject highlighted by this unknown preacher was the false assumption held by many believers that listening to the message of the gospel is enough to be illumined by it. Agreeing, Tozer likewise corrects this false notion by stating that if the voice of God does not speak within, the mind cannot be illumined. The Spirit of God must speak quietly in the interior of a person, for this is what reels us in and makes us responsible before God. The words of the text falling on a human ear can mean absolutely nothing.[54]

Returning briefly to the case of Paul's conversion, we can assume that Paul's appointment with the Lord on the road to Damascus had such a strong effect on him because he had already been immersed in the study of the Scriptures, albeit in an incomplete way. The same diligent study of the Scriptures that had created a cognitive environment in Paul that proved so favorable for his particularly deep reception of the gospel, however, only *became* revelation for him once he personally encountered the risen word. It was this mystical, existential event that opened his eyes to see Jesus Christ as the hermeneutical key to the whole of Scripture (1 Cor 15:3–4; cf. Luke 24:31–32).

54. Tozer, *Ten Sermons*, 62.

Chapter 3

Pneumatolatry
Making an Idol of the Spirit of God

INTRODUCTION TO PNEUMATOLATRY

[A] theology that views doctrine in relation to the reality that doctrine aims to articulate is a theology that relates experience to the production of knowledge. When doctrine speaks its truth, it speaks of experience.[1]

Just as spirituality has something to say about doctrine, doctrine also has something to say about spirituality.[2]

If a genuine Christ encounter is required for the Bible to be the word of God *for us* in its fullest sense, then the Spirit of God must be central to all that the Bible and Bible reading is. Indeed, the Spirit's operations in inspiration and illumination come together in the communication of God's word to the creature: inspiration in forming the canonical texts as revealed truth and illumination in making that truth alive through the believing, obedient reading of those texts. Christ through the Spirit is present throughout. At whatever point of the hermeneutical cycle the Spirit is missing, so is Christ.

---

1. Helmer, *Theology and the End of Doctrine*, 7.
2. Stephenson, "Role of Spirituality," 89.

Pneumatolatry

If, therefore, the Holy Spirit plays such a decisive role in all things related to the Bible, it should come as no surprise to discover throughout Scripture a language denoting Spirit experiences of God's people. As demonstrated in the previous chapter, this is indeed what we find. A doctrinalist approach, however, often finds itself attempting to downplay such language amidst concern that the more Christians focus on the experiential side of the Spirit's work, the less likely they are to concentrate on the more surefooted, rationally-grounded doctrinal aspects.[3] Often this concern has resulted in a reductionistic and reactionary—some would say obscurantist or alarmist—rejection for fear of all things experiential.[4] Notwithstanding such disproportionate responses, a sober warning remains to be given. Despite the sincere desire to know God in a more personal and tangible way, many experientialist communities tend towards a concept of Christian spirituality—that is, the knowledge of God that unites us savingly to God's life—as a series of fleeting emotional experiences, often reaching a crescendo in physical or near-physical experiences of the divine being.

That the search for experiences of God is primary in many groups is clearly seen in the increasingly common philosophy of the "worship meeting." To avoid gatherings perceived of as "dead," many communities have established a form of worship that essentially consists in a prolonged heart-invocation of the Holy Spirit. The driving hope behind this kind of meeting is that the Spirit might descend upon the congregation in power in order to accompany believers into God's glorious presence. This access into the presence of God is confirmed through heightened emotions among the believers and a sense of wonder caused by the tangible manifestations of the Spirit in their midst. Prophecies, miracles, healings, demon exorcisms, and the like are often telltale signs that the wall between heaven and earth has been breached. The effects of such experiences last for the duration of the worship meeting and for a short time afterwards, then fade away, segueing

---

3. There are examples both ancient and contemporary of this concern by the church. Writing of the ancient restorationist charismatic movement called Montanism, Jaroslav Pelikan, for example, explains how its fixation with "new prophets" pushed the church catholic of the time to recognize "its inevitable need for fixed forms of dogma and creed" (Pelikan, *Emergence of the Catholic Tradition*, 107). The similar contemporary situation will be alluded to throughout the chapter.

4. Urban Holmes III refers to what he calls "Extrinsic religion," which is fundamentally defensive in character. "It encourages the person to exclude others and may even breed a kind of paranoia, as exemplified in the mass suicides of the People's Temple in Guyana in November of 1978. Its greatest enemy is risk" (Holmes, *A History of Christian Spirituality*, 6).

into anticipation of the next meeting, where it is hoped the Spirit will once again manifest in this same way.

The establishment of this liturgical form has produced a generation of believers who increasingly seek God at their own convenience (i.e., in the experiences they can have of him in meetings or in other particular circumstances). Here worship is an event rather than a way of life, a feeling rather than a renewed mind-set. Here believers risk having their joy derived from delight in the worship process itself rather than in the Lord for the Lord's sake. Largely foreign to this approach is the notion of worship of the Worthy *worthily*. According to Ralph P. Martin, worship is "the dramatic celebration of God in his supreme worth in such a manner that his 'worthiness' becomes the norm and inspiration of human living."[5] The view of worthy worship as rooted in discipleship is highlighted by Isaiah's polemic against Judah's *worthless* worship due to Judah's superficiality in following the ordinances of the Lord (Isa 1:11–17). From the noble and arduous call to be worshipping disciples, many self-designated worshippers today are little more than diligent devotees of the spectacular.

Such worship can easily slip into exploitation, insofar as it seeks to procure "abracadabra moments" of the Holy Spirit for personal enjoyment. While God is indeed to be greatly enjoyed through the operation of the Spirit in the gathered church, he is to be enjoyed spiritually and not in the fleshly manner of a spectator at a parade. Of course, the line can be fine at times, but Christ-minded believers can generally discern the spirit of genuine worship from manufactured adulation.

Nonetheless, the fabricated approach to worship so common today has obviously struck a chord, for it attracts professing Christians in droves. While also endorsed and conducted by sincere Christian leaders, false prophets and teachers adept at exploiting the drawing power of the Holy Spirit often slip through our defenses and establish themselves in places of prominence. While they draw thousands or even hundreds of thousands, their excesses scare off a great many openhearted believers from seeking an authentic, deeper experiential relationship with God. This dynamic is symptomatic of what I call "pneumatolatry."[6]

---

5. Martin, *Worship of God*, 4. I have assumed Martin's affirmation as my working definition of "worship."

6. I do not associate this term with any specific denomination or movement. I intend it, rather, as a phenomenon that cuts across boundaries and can occur anywhere, even if in fact it is more common in certain groups than in others. NB: The term is to be distinguished from the systematic theological study of the Holy Spirit commonly known

Pneumatolatry

From *pneuma*, the Greek word for "spirit," together with "idolatry," this neologism at first glance appears to be an oxymoron, for the Holy Spirit is truly God, and therefore by definition cannot be idolized. However, I use the term in a technical sense to refer to a certain kind of *spirituality* based on the assumption that the only true knowledge we can have of God is through experiencing him. This notion mistrusts emphasis on the intellectual pursuit of comprehending biblical teaching as a genuine means of knowing God spiritually. At the same time, it has a reductionistic view of Christian experience, associating it mainly with feelings produced by worshipping and especially worshipping with a pre-defined, expected range of manifestations of the Holy Spirit.

In contrast to the neutral notion of "Spiritualized" treated in this book's introduction, pneumatolatry has a decidedly negative connotation. It is a spirituality that *narrowly identifies the knowledge of God that unites us to God with palpable experiences of the wonder-working Holy Spirit*. On the one hand, this view borders on exploitation of the Holy Spirit for the purpose of fulfilling the worshipper's desires for emotional religious experiences. On the other, it is a conceptual corruption of the relationship between the Father, the Son, and the Holy Spirit. Simply put, it is a kind of idolatry of the Holy Spirit that tampers with the glory of the Trinity, being altered, as it were, *from* and *for* the flesh (cf. Rom 1:23).

THE ORDER OF WORSHIP OF THE TRIUNE GOD

Theological Groundings

In the Scriptures, God reveals himself as the one God of Israel, who at the same time is also three: Father, Son, and Holy Spirit. Neither the oneness nor the threeness of God is ever compromised, so we are bound to conclude along with the tradition that God's tri-unity is in its fullness an unknowable mystery, even though it has been revealed to the degree that it accords with God's measure and purposes.

Jesus is very clear about the hierarchy that exists in God's redemptive revelation of himself when he declares that the Father is greater than he is (John 14:28; cf. 1 Cor 15:28). Of Christ, on the other hand, it is written that he "is all and in all" (Col 3:11) and that "all things were created through him and for him" (Col 1:16). These are assertions that are never predicated

---

as "pneumatology."

on the Holy Spirit, for instance. Furthermore, it is the Father who sends the Son, and it is the Son who goes and returns, asking that the Spirit be sent in his place. It is the Son who dies—not the Father or the Spirit—but it is the Father, through the power of the Spirit, who raises the Son from the dead. Finally, when the Son and the Spirit's missions will have been completed, the Son will give all he has received back to God in blessed obedience and submission (1 Cor 15:28). Thus, God has revealed himself *economically*—in his operations towards the world—as hierarchical and, in a manner, functionally specialized.

Systematic theologians, however, do not only speak of the economic Trinity, they also refer to God's *ontological* or *immanent* tri-unity—that is, God as Father, Son, and Spirit as he is in himself, *ad intra*, outside of time and space, apart from his work of creation and redemption. There is currently a discussion among theologians concerning whether it is also proper to speak of a hierarchy within the immanent Trinity—that is, whether the Son and the Spirit are in some way subordinate to the Father, even in God's eternal inner being apart from how he has manifested himself in redemption.[7] This is not the place to expound upon such things beyond mentioning them.

That which concerns us presently, rather, is the practical applications of how our understandings of the Trinitarian God influence how we worship him. In what way is this a practical concern? For example, if we bracket God's revelation of himself in the world and understand the Trinity's inner nature as devoid of hierarchy, then the playing field is leveled, as it were, and there is no theological justification prohibiting us from addressing the three Persons of the Godhead interchangeably and indiscriminately in prayer, song, teaching, or worship. If, on the other hand, our approach is towards God's immanence and we also understand the Father, Son, and Spirit to be related hierarchically from eternity, then reverence for the divine order would summon us to grasp the differences between the divine

---

7. This debate within Trinitarian theology is referred to as EFS, which stands for "Eternal Functional Subordination." The central point argued is whether the Son's functional subordination to the Father is restricted only to the economic Trinity or extends to the ontological Trinity so that it may be stated that the Son is functionally subordinate to the Father not only in his incarnated state, but also in his hypostatical being from all eternity. It should be noted that the opponents to EFS see in this position a form of tritheism, while pro-EFS theologians counter that they avoid this heresy by claiming that the eternal subordination of the Son is always ever "functional" and not "ontological"—i.e., not having to do with the Son's essential nature. See, for example, Johnson, "Trinitarian Agency," esp. 7n1.

persons before we haphazardly decide to treat all three persons uniformly in our worship.

Whatever we might believe about God's immanent being, it is clear that God has revealed himself hierarchically in his operations *towards us*—that is, economically. I would argue that as a model for our practical worship, we should turn above all to the economic Trinity because of its clarity, emphasis, and practicality in Scripture.[8] To put it another way, I think a proper practical theology of spirituality most suitably starts in God as he has revealed himself in his saving activity rather than by what we can surmise speculatively about his ontological being.[9] Summing up, if worship in truth and spirit is ultimately a practical exercise that derives from our knowledge and acknowledgement of who God is, then it appears to me that for our understanding of worship, we should lean most heavily on the economic Trinity simply because this is how God has most fully revealed himself to us so we might know and worship him (e.g., Matt 11:27; 16:17; John 1:31; 14:17; Eph 3:4–5).

It would be the task of a far more technical book to expound on these questions in any depth. For the present purposes, I will simply state what I recognize in Scripture as that understanding of the Trinitarian God that is most relevant for our worship. I will then use this brief synopsis as the basis of a critique of notions of worship within contemporary evangelical experientialism. I will support my position implicitly throughout the rest of the chapter.

---

8. This does not mean that I understand the immanent and economic Trinities as irreconcilably polarized or that I collapse the ontological into the economic Trinity, as Karl Rahner famously did. In the important work of the evangelical theologian Bruce McCormack, a *post-metaphysical* case is made for an eternal subordination within the immanent Trinity that connects it organically to the economic Trinity without, however succumbing to either of the aforementioned extremes. For a concise though dense presentation of his view, see McCormack, "Processions Contain the Missions."

9. The question of the relationship between God's inner and economic beings is highly contested today. The situation has notably taken shape as a dispute between Trinitarians such as Jürgen Moltmann, John Zizioulas, and Miroslav Volf, who advocate a view that God's immanent being in some authentic sense mirrors the personal relationality of his economic being, and Pro-Nicene Trinitarians such as Michele René Barnes, Lewis Ayres, and Stephen Holmes, who claim that patristic Trinitarianism was united in its claim that the relations of the persons of God *ad intra* are not personal in the same sense we get from the economic Trinity. For both theological and philosophical presentations of the contemporary debate see Maspero and Wozniak, *Rethinking Trinitarian Theology*; McCall and Rea, *Philosophical and Theological Essays*; Schwöbel, *Trinitarian Theology Today*.

DOCTRINE AND EXPERIENCE

We worship only one God, and we worship him for who he is as revealed by what he has done for us—that is, in accordance to how he has revealed himself to be in his operations towards the world. This leads us to deduce that how God has revealed himself in creation and redemption is in some authentic sense who he must be in himself from eternity. Otherwise, how could we claim to worship him in truth? From a phenomenological perspective, I do not think we can deduce otherwise, though theoretically there are many fine distinctions we need to make if we are to avoid caricature. Scripture reveals elements of both the immanent and the economic Trinity, though it has far more to say concerning the latter. This overwhelming emphasis on the economic being of God points to the Spirit's purpose of inspiring a Scripture that provides us with a practical spirituality. Even though we are told certain things concerning God as he is in himself, and although we are able to deduce still more, no reasonable theologian would ever claim that we could therefore know God's being fully in his eternal, inaccessible light. Certainly, we could not imitate this aspect of God in practical discipleship. However, as already noted, the special revelation of Scripture is quite exhaustive in what it has to say about God economically (though humility and wisdom oblige us to consider that probably even this revelation is selective). Furthermore, since the purpose of special revelation is expressly stated as existing for the edification of the church, and since worship is an integral part of this building up, it would appear that we are to take our cue concerning true spiritual worship principally from how God has revealed himself in his concrete operations of creation and redemption rather than as he might be according to our calculated inferences of his being *ad intra*.

When we bow down before God, we worship he whom we have known in the face of Jesus Christ through the Holy Spirit. To do otherwise would be to bow down before a reconstructed God of theoretical Trinitarian theology. The latter can and has historically sometimes degenerated into idolatry. The very fact of the incarnation, however, would appear to point us in a more pragmatic direction for understanding worship. Such spiritual worship is grounded in a knowledge of the radiance of his glory (Heb 1:1)—that is, his Son, who, "though he was in the form of God ... made himself nothing ... being born in the likeness of men" (Phil 2:6–8). This is the *same* Jesus who was born of a virgin, was reared in Northern Israel, rose from the dead, and ascended back to the Father to pour out the Holy Spirit on all flesh, taking his place as our eternal high priest at the right hand of the heavenly throne and there waits until he is told to return. In other words, we bow down before the God who has revealed himself in creation and redemption as a hierarchy of persons with differing roles and functions.

It is from this vantage point that I urge fear and trembling in our order of worship. In contemporary evangelicalism, this warning is particularly relevant to how we treat the person of the Holy Spirit in worship. On the one hand, in view of what we know about God, any worship that relegates the Holy Spirit to little more than an afterthought is indeed bound to be lacking and wrongheaded. The church is compelled by Scripture and experience to welcome the Spirit as a fully designated person, to desire his fullness, seek his gifts, his counsel, his direction, and his comfort by submitting wholly to his will, for he is revealed as the true God and so is worthy of our worship and praise. What the church is not authorized to do, however, is to arbitrarily establish the Spirit in positions and functions—according to our own agendas—that do not belong to him within the divine economy. This is the essence of my theological critique of pneumatolatry as it is found in much contemporary evangelical experientialism.

A Call to Theological Propriety in Worship

While I believe a response to pneumatolatry is needed, my critique is neither reactionary nor anti-charismatic per se. Nevertheless, I am well aware that taken at face value, my statements above can give the opposite impression. Therefore, I will reframe my position in terms of an appeal for theological propriety in worship.[10]

I believe that pneumatolatry is careless and often irreverent in its practical insistence that our experiences may trump God's written revelation

---

10. This point has been addressed in the controversial "Strange Fire" conference in October of 2013. Contrary to what certain portions of my argument might suggest, I do not align myself with this movement in which high-profile leaders like John MacArthur and R. C. Sproul denounce the Pentecostal and charismatic movements seemingly without discrimination. While no doubt carried forth in good conscience, the tone of the critique is flippant at times, with the kind of in-house, tongue-in-cheek banter that suggests a private club mentality and a cessationist agenda going beyond the right Christian desire to warn against and correct error. Having said this, however, I think that many of the points the conference criticizes do indeed need to be critically, ethically, and theologically examined and, in some cases, condemned. Since my own position converges at times with certain points highlighted by the conference, I thought it best to state my position as clearly as possible from the outset.

of himself as binding for how we should worship God. While doctrine is indeed dead without genuine experience of God, our experiences must ultimately always be borne up by right doctrine. Why else would the Spirit who inspired the Scriptures "go out of his way" to stress the importance of truth for the Spirit-filled life (see John 4:24). To shove Trinitarian doctrine flippantly aside in our spiritual formation mocks the God who has revealed himself as a hierarchy in his operations towards the world. The exaltation of the manifestations of the Holy Spirit as the end-all of worship misunderstands the Deity, because the Holy Spirit "proceeds from the Father" (John 15:26) and not the other way around. Pneumatolatry is wrong, therefore, not because it exalts the Holy Spirit but because it minimizes the importance of the roles and functions of the persons of the Trinity in God's economy by viewing these doctrines as suffocating rather than liberating.

When we make the Holy Spirit the centerpiece of our worship by dedicating more time to his person and actions than to Jesus Christ, we demonstrate that we do not know the Spirit we claim to be worshipping. In the same way as it is proper to worship, praise, and honor the Son because he is God, so too is the worship of the Spirit welcome and right. However, we must worship him for who he is and for what he chooses to be in obedience to the Father—namely, the "John the Baptist" of the Trinity, whose mission on the earth is to obey the Father by pointing us to Christ and then to retire, so to speak, into the background.[11] Even the distribution of gifts, healings, miracles, and dealings with demons point us to Christ's cross, for though they are all accomplished in the power of the Spirit, the Spirit is single-mindedly fixed on building up the church by making the gospel of Jesus Christ real to believers through their experience. That the Spirit should be so humble notwithstanding his great power should not surprise us, for the Son of Man also fully embraced a subordinate position in the economy of God to the Father (John 4:34; 6:38) and even understood his own glory in terms of that submission (John 8:54; 17:24). It can be argued, of course, that Jesus drew attention to himself as the mediator in the flesh between humanity and God. However, this is what the Father specifically sent him to do; he understood this attention as the necessary means of uniting lost sinners to the Father's life, in accordance with his mission. The Spirit's ministry is different; he has no mandate to draw people to himself.

Unfortunately, the Holy Spirit is often "the forgotten man" in much contemporary evangelical life and worship, to say nothing of the historical

---

11. Cf. John 1:20 with 15:26 and John 3:30 with 16:13–14.

Pneumatolatry

Protestant movement in general. Clearly, this should not be the case; it is a serious mistake to fail to recognize publicly and often the Spirit of God at work in the assembly. The Spirit is personal and lovable in himself, and not all believers seek to know the Spirit as a real person to be loved and adored for who he is. Precisely because we want to worship him for who he is, we need to ask what ministry the Spirit has been given and has chosen to uphold in the church and world in obedience to the Father. What does the Spirit reveal about all this?

First, worship is not above all offered *to* the Spirit but *through* him so that we can boast in Christ and not in ourselves (Phil 3:3). The Spirit is the glorious and great God, but in the divine economy, he is the means by which the Son is exalted amongst God's people. In fact, we can assert on the basis of Scripture that the Spirit's main purpose in the economy of God is to celebrate Jesus. Indeed, only if the Son is celebrated is the Spirit honored. Whenever we celebrate the Spirit at the expense of the Son, the Spirit is dishonored, for he was sent to draw us to Christ and not to himself. From the perspective of experience, it is useless to even argue the point, for when the church is genuinely under the guidance of the Spirit, its gaze is naturally fixed on the person and work of Christ such that the question of who should be the object of worship is not even brought up. One wonders who is leading the worship when the cross of Christ is nearly forgotten and the manifestations of the Spirit are given center stage. It is beyond doubt that in such worship there is more flesh than Spirit.

It is important, therefore, that the disciple of Christ should strive to be in harmony with *God's* ways of doing things. Making the Spirit and his works the center of meetings is something the Spirit himself does not desire, for he proceeded from the Father precisely to testify to the glory of the Son (John 15:26; 16:14) so that the Father might be glorified in the Christ (John 17:1). If we really want to be worshipers of God, we must learn to worship him in spirit and in truth. This means, among other things, that worshipers need to stop calling spiritualities informed by human innovation and natural desire scriptural, as if they have been taught by the Holy Spirit rather than by men and women who learn what it is to worship God more from their own interpretations of personal experiences than from inspired biblical doctrine.

If the precise order of God's being and actions seem trivial to some, we might apply, somewhat out of context, Paul's words to Israel: "But who are you, O man, to answer back to God?" (Rom 9:20). We might also say,

"Do not be deceived: God is not mocked, for whatever one sows, that will he also reap" (Gal 6:7). In the Old Testament, the propriety of worship was of fundamental importance. It was to be carried out in the tabernacle or temple by sanctified priests and not by any other person, unless specifically indicated by the Lord. To move even modestly from this revealed order to establish one's own instruction for worship was literally to play with fire, for those who acted in this way were to be put to death (Num 1:51; 3:10, 3:38, 18:7; Deut 16:21–17:6). It was indeed dangerous for the Israelite to decide for himself or herself how to worship God, because it was presumptuous. Anyone who offered "strange fire" upon God's altar—that is, whoever worshiped according to his or her own canon of truth and not God's—risked ending up like the sons of Aaron, who were called specifically to the task of worshipping. It should serve as a reminder that Nadab and Abihu's end came by way of God's true fire from heaven devouring them for their presumption concerning false fire (Lev 10:1–2; Num 3:4).

I do not wish to make a blanket condemnation of everyone who confuses God's order of things at some point, for then nobody in all the church would be left standing. It is also true that the New Testament is significantly quiet on matters concerning how to worship publically, indicating that there is probably a great deal of freedom in the matter. Nevertheless, there is certainly a progression concerning the nature and person of God as we pass from the Old Testament to the New. With this new revelation comes a more complete understanding of true worship. We are obliged to do our best to get in line with what God has made known, for the alternative is to conform to our own creaturely inventions. There is no middle ground.

My reasoning, therefore, is as follows: if my way of worshipping God is not in accordance with how God has revealed himself to us, then it is according to either human or diabolical invention. When I am careless in this regard, I find that I am more like Cain than Abel. Both made sacrifices to the Lord, but only Abel's was accepted. Cain's was not of faith (Heb 11:4) but of sight, and so it was fleshly. Cain was guilty of methodological idolatry, worshipping the true God but in his own way—the way of the creature without knowledge or faith.

When our worship winds up centered more on the experiences of the Holy Spirit than on the work and Person of Christ, we can be certain we have turned the third Person of the Trinity into an image of our own making—one that does not and cannot represent the true God. When we do this to revel in certain *charismata* (gifts) and manifestations of the Spirit, we only confirm that we are seeking to satisfy our fleshly cravings and not allowing the Holy Spirit to act freely at all. Should the Spirit want to manifest signs and wonders, bring about tears and wailing, permit healings or miracles, then so be it. But should he desire for God's people to worship in silent meditation, Bible reading, doctrinal discourse, or hushed prayer and inward praise, he should also be free to do that. Who is in charge, after all? No less controlling, of course, is the a priori prohibition of a more charged atmosphere for our worship. Wherever we do not submit to the Spirit's leading but instead expect this or that kind of worship experience, we exploit the Holy Spirit for our own traditions or preferences rather than submitting to his work, which is to glorify Jesus Christ and convict us of our lowliness according to his own sovereign directives (1 Cor 12:11).

If my reasoning is sound, then much experientialist worship exposes a lack of faith. The wonders of God do indeed abound, and he still does wonderful things in our midst according to his grace, but an evil generation actively seeks experiences for their own sake.

PUT UP OR SHUT UP

> Now we have received not the spirit of the world, but the Spirit who is from God, that we might understand the things freely given us by God. And we impart this in words not taught by human wisdom but taught by the Spirit, interpreting spiritual truths to those who are spiritual.[12]

> But I, brothers, could not address you as spiritual people, but as people of the flesh, as infants in Christ.[13]

Two thousand years ago, the Apostle Paul faced a situation in the church of Corinth that was similar to ours in several respects. The Corinthian believers had the wrong idea about what constitutes the worship of God. The tragic element of the history of this church is that it had been particularly blessed with many gifts (1 Cor 1:5–7). However, because of the Corinthian believers' immaturity, abuses were rampant. This carnal-mindedness manifested in various ways. One of the greatest excesses was the practice among believers to speak in a way that seemed to be spiritual but was in truth fleshly.

---

12. 1 Cor 2:12–13.
13. 1 Cor 3:1.

DOCTRINE AND EXPERIENCE

The passages cited above show that, for Paul, the Spirit teaches a genuine spiritual talk. For it to be truly spiritual, however, such talk has to correspond to "spiritual truths" and be received by "spiritual people." In the context of First Corinthians, these truths do not refer either to special giftedness or to great knowledge or to religious standing but rather to a holy and pious life characterized above all else by self-sacrificial love in contrast to self-seeking (1 Cor 13:1–3). For even if Paul is writing about the Spirit's revelation of a "secret and hidden wisdom" of God in Christ (1 Cor 2:7), he makes it more than clear that the Corinthians are too fleshly to receive such things (1 Cor 3:1). In the words of the apostle, truly spiritual words are only for the truly spiritually minded (1 Cor 2:13). It is also clear that for Paul, the Corinthian believers were not living this reality, despite the demonstration of the gifts in their midst. For this reason, their use of spiritual words was in reality a mere form of godliness without the power of God (cf. 2 Tim 3:5).

We can infer that this was indeed the situation in Corinth from several different reproaches Paul scattered throughout the letter. For example, the church was driven by personality cults, probably centered on who was baptized by which famous representative faction in the community (1 Cor 1:14). As a result, different groups of believers made certain assertions aimed at demonstrating each group's elite spiritual standing: "I follow Paul," "I follow Apollos," "I follow Cephas," and "I follow Christ" (1 Cor 1:12). But Paul exposed the very statements the believers thought validated their spiritual reputations as instead carnal, immature, and childlike (1 Cor 3:4). In the final analysis, such talk was nothing but empty boastings of vain believers (1 Cor 3:21). Indeed, their boasts did not stop with who was of Paul, Apollo, or Cephas. They actually boasted of having "arrived" spiritually ahead of some of those very leaders (1 Cor 4:7–8). And that was not all. They celebrated their own gifts of the Holy Spirit while the worst of sins went unaddressed and even condoned in their midst (1 Cor 5:1–6). They were the original pneumatolaters, making their personal experiences and the gifts of the Spirit the measure of spirituality while simultaneously (and consequently) showing little concern for God's order of things.

As if using their spiritual words in order to prop up their own reputation was not bad enough, these believers were guilty of doing the same with words that came straight down from heaven. I refer to the problem in Corinth concerning speaking in tongues. Paul did not rebuke the Corinthians because they spoke in tongues but because they fitted these spiritual words to unspiritual "truths"—that is, to an individualism that rushed

Pneumatolatry

headlong into selfishness and empty boasting (1 Cor 14:9). In fact, when Paul wrote that he would ascertain not the "talk" of the so-called spiritual people but their "power" (1 Cor 4:19), he was basically challenging them to "put up or shut up."[14]

As Raymond Brown comments, whenever the apostle resorts to the authoritarian "bottom line," we can be certain we are dealing with a difficult subject.[15] Those who would like to recover for their own lives the charismatic reality found in certain New Testament passages would therefore do well to take Paul's exhortation to the Corinthians seriously:

> If anyone thinks he is a prophet or spiritual, let him recognize that the things which I write to you are the Lord's commandment. If anyone does not recognize this, he is not recognized. (1 Cor 14:37–38)

As history teaches us, it takes very little to pass from true spirituality to a hyped-up, boastful, ultra-triumphalist form of spirituality.[16] It was for this reason that Paul reminded the Corinthian believers that when he visited them, it was "in weakness and in fear and much trembling," having decided not to strut in with lofty words of spiritual grandeur "but in demonstration of the Spirit and of power" (1 Cor 2:1–5).

Paul adopted this strategy because he knew something that neither the Corinthian believers nor many Christians today have understood—namely that "the kingdom of God does not consist in talk but in power" (1 Cor 4:20) and that this power is manifested supremely in the weakness of the cross (1 Cor 2:2–3) rather than in boastful speeches concerning great works done, seen, or desired. Paul's argument is to be interpreted in light of the immediate context: that of the alleged spirituality of people whose speech appeared powerful to the naked ear but was weak and ineffective to those who had ears to hear (1 Cor 4:18).

EVERYONE WHO ASKS RECEIVES

In our times, things are not very different among those whose main understanding of spirituality is a reliving of certain experiences read about in the

---

14. Perhaps Paul was referring to those of Second Corinthians, who had said that in his letters Paul was powerful in word but was weak in person (2 Cor 10:10).

15. Brown, *Introduction to the New Testament*, 531.

16. Or, for that matter, to a dead, uncharitable, legalistic faith. See Galatians.

Gospels and Acts. In church gatherings, big and small, it is common to hear what amounts to a formalized "spiritual" language consisting of invocations for the Holy Spirit to come down and reproduce the apostolic glory of God in the assembly and beyond. Such "glory" is often envisioned in terms of a select variety of "signs and wonders" as well as feelings of elation and awe. Based on the carnal mind-set of many, however, one is inclined to believe that what often passes for pleas of divine spiritual power are really examples of talking to the wind.

I realize this is both a generalized and difficult statement, but if we are really interested in knowing the power of God, we must look critically not only at how our "worship vocabulary" works itself out in our behavior both inside and outside the church, but also at the fruit it produces as regards answered prayer.

> For everyone who asks receives... (Luke 11:10a)

If the words we use correspond to spiritual reality, we can take this promise of Christ at face value. However, when this is not the case we should not expect our prayers to be answered, and the promise mutates into a warning about the vain use of spiritual-sounding words that are disconnected from spiritual truths. Significantly, it is precisely in this discourse in Luke where Jesus promises the Holy Spirit or true spirituality to all who would ask the Father (Luke 11:13).[17] If we take the Lord's assurance seriously, we have a substantial argument in favor of the following hypothesis: a lack of specific, concrete responses to requests for signs and wonders suggests that the words being used do not correspond to a genuine spiritual reality. In colloquial terms, if we find ourselves continually asking for certain manifestations of the Spirit in our lives, our families, and our churches, yet we do not receive that which we ask for, it is likely that we are talking to the wind.

By making such a claim, I do not deny that God still does shake the foundations of buildings, not to mention the gates of hell, with mighty power in answer to our prayers (Acts 4:31; cf. 12:7; 16:26). Revival power, however, especially in Acts and Paul, appears to be the response to a singularly motivated request—namely, that the disciples might continue boldly in the service of preaching the cross of Christ. While God does answer with wonders, which consequently results in praise and adoration—and in the

---

17. This verse can also be interpreted to mean that the good heavenly Father gives *spiritual blessings* to those who ask him (cf. the parallel text in Matt 7:11 and also Rom 8:32). See, for example, Carson et al., "Luke 11:1–13," in *New Bible Commentary*.

Pneumatolatry

case of Acts 16:26, is caused by it—the disciples never conceived of asking for the Spirit as a means of experiencing wonders, in order to increase the quality or intensity of their "worship services." The filling of the Spirit with this kind of power was always and only a means to serve the cause of the cross more effectively. Moreover, God always answered *this* prayer, just as Jesus had promised, whereas the asking for signs and wonders of many pneumatolaters go unanswered.[18]

Of course when inquiring as to the reasons for unanswered prayer of any kind, we also need to consider other factors. For example, we need to reflect on the Lord's sovereign timing in responding to our pleas, not to mention his desire that we learn patience, constancy, and perseverance in our prayer life. Jesus' statement that all who ask receive therefore has to be supplemented not only by many other teachings, but also by the previous verse and the remainder of the same verse (Luke 11:9 and 10 b, c). Surely, the triplet of "ask," "seek," and "knock" in verse 9 followed by the promises of fulfillment in verse 10 suggest perseverance in prayer, so we should learn to "keep at it" rather than expect everything to drop immediately into our laps. However, the point I want to make presently is to be understood in the context of asking for signs, miracles, wonders, healings, and other charismatic manifestations of the Holy Spirit as the *normative content* of our prayers and, as a result, our lives.

Earnestly Desire the Gifts . . . But First the Cross!

The question of what is normative for the Christian life is in many respects the boundary line issue dividing charismatics and non-charismatics. The former take for granted that the life of Jesus and the apostles as presented in the Gospels and Acts should be normative in all its wonder-working intensity; the latter gain their understanding of what is normative much more from a reading of explicit teaching laid out in the gospels and epistles.

Important for the question at hand is that in the New Testament there is relatively little if any explicit instruction concerning contemporary experientialist charismatic distinctives. It is necessary to walk a fine line here, as it is undesirable that Scripture should be pitted against itself in the questions

---

18. For the present, I am bracketing hyper-fringe groups who believe they receive everything they ask for despite the evidence to the contrary. Moderate experientialists also rightly criticize such extremists for lacking in discernment as to what really constitutes God's presence in power.

of truth and practice. Personally, I would take a *via media*. The Gospels and Acts serve as a very general model for the *kind* of kingdom power available for the church today, but the emphasis of our Christian lives should reflect what was most stressed by Christ and the apostles—namely, their instruction in doctrine and practice.

Perhaps a good place to start for demonstrating this thesis would be the complementary passages of 1 Cor 12:31 and 14:1:

> But earnestly desire the higher gifts. And I will show you a still more excellent way.

> Pursue love, and earnestly desire the spiritual gifts, especially that you may prophesy.

It is clear from both verses that Paul valued sacrificial love over gifts and valued gifts that were useful for the entire body over those geared for personal edification.[19] While God is glorified in the practice of his gifts in the church, given the elitism being dealt with in Corinth, it is improbable that Paul was encouraging the believers to seek the greater gifts for their own sake. It seems this had been one of the roots of the problem in the first place. More by way of concession than as a prime directive, Paul urges the Corinthians to eagerly desire the greater gifts. For him, the gifts had value only in relation to how they were practiced within a cross-shaped community. Then, as now, the elevation of the gifts to a place of prominence without the efficacious working of the cross in the assembly is a major cause of snobbery and divisiveness. Raymond Brown's wise warning to the contemporary charismatic movement is in line with this thought when he writes, "Modern appreciation of charisms sometimes neglects the fact that they were very divisive at Corinth. Inevitably, whether a charism or an office is involved, when one Christian claims to have a role others do not have, issues of superiority and envy are introduced."[20]

Whatever precisely Paul meant by "desiring the greater gifts," one thing is clear—the purpose of his discourse on the gifts in chapters 12 through 14 was not to promote the miraculous amongst the believers but the cross resulting in love. Paul's sections on unity in diversity (12), love (13), and

---

19. The exegesis of 1 Cor 12:31a is a much debated issue amongst scholars, and there are various views on how to understand of the verse. For the terms of the debate, see Fee, *First Epistle to the Corinthians*; Perkins, *First Corinthians*; Fitzmeyer, *First Corinthians*; Thiselton, *First Epistle to the Corinthians*.

20. Brown, *Introduction to the New Testament*, 532.

Pneumatolatry

intelligibility and order (14) all amount to a call for the Corinthian believers to strive above all for a cross-centered worship in which each member would lay aside self for the good of the entire body as well as for possible visitors. This is the foundation on which a worthy worship must be built, and it is precisely what is missing in much experientialist spirituality today. I would argue that it is noteworthy that the main body of teaching God has left his church on the gifts is there primarily to criticize those who were practicing them in the flesh and not according to the Spirit. While this may be true of a number of issues in the New Testament, it does suggest that for Paul the cross was to be desired more eagerly than the gifts. Indeed, we can deduce from this that no matter how powerfully the gifts of the Spirit at Corinth were actually exercised, they were nevertheless impotent to do good because the cross was not present to make them spiritual in an inclusive way (1 Cor 3:1).

Consequently, there appears to be two varieties of power in the kingdom: that which we see in some of the gifts and might term "manifest power" as well as a greater, more worthy *veiled power* seen in the working of the cross. To concentrate on the first while neglecting the second is both sinful and counterproductive. Where there is no cross, there is no sanctification and thus unabated sin. This is the case no matter how many gifts are being practiced. Furthermore, without the cross, true resurrection power is stunted. Indeed, wherever the cross is marginalized the manifest power of the gifts becomes a negative power, spiritually speaking (see 1 Cor 1–3). Where the cross is at work, however, the manifest power of the gifts will accomplish what they were designed to achieve. Where the cross is absent, the effectiveness of the gifts will be reduced to the clanging of a noisy gong, unpleasing to God.

Thus, the discourse on gifts in First Corinthians really only serves as the context for highlighting what is really central to Paul's ecclesiology—as with all his theology—namely, the cross at work in the world to undergird the church as it forges fallen human beings into Christ's image. Undeniably, everything in the New Testament—worship, gifts, signs and wonders, church order, piety, doctrine, creation, Israelite history, and salvation itself—is viewed in the towering shadow of the cross of Christ. For this reason, Jesus was hesitant to allow those who experienced his miraculous powers to divulge the arrival of the kingdom (Mark 5:43) and proclaim him king (John 6:15) before (a) he fulfilled the will of his Father on Calvary and (b) the disciples started understanding the cross in their own lives (Matt

26:75; cf. John 21:17–18; see also Acts 14:22). In this way, the Holy Spirit indicates that the supernatural workings of the Messiah, without the activity of the cross, only serve to lead people into false spirituality.

We can see this even in two "hostile" passages to this thesis, in which it appears that Paul asks God for *manifest power* without reference to the cross. I have in mind the two prayers in Ephesians. In the first prayer, Paul asks that the Ephesians might know by experience the immeasurable greatness of God's power (Eph 1:21). This appeal is sometimes seen as paradigmatic for the contemporary church's pursuit of signs and wonders. But Paul only makes this request because he recognized the profound effects of the cross already at work in the believers' lives through their faith and sacrificial love for the saints (Eph 1:15). Otherwise, it is doubtful that Paul would have prayed like this. In the second prayer, Paul asks the Father that the believers might be strengthened with power through his Spirit in their inner being (Eph 3:16). This prayer is sometimes taken out of context to mean "Strengthened with power to perform mighty deeds." For Paul, however, the goal of this power was that the Spirit of the self-sacrificing Christ might dwell in their hearts by faith in order to produce in them the same sacrificial love. In these two requests, we see that for Paul cross-shaped love is both the condition for and effect of God's power in and through the church.

Just as it was for the Corinthian believers, this understanding is also lost on the modern-day pneumatolater. The establishment of the pursuit of God's manifest power as the major or even sole duty of spirituality changes the goal of Christianity from imitation of the humility of Christ (Phil 2:5) to replication of Christ's experience of the miraculous. Those who practice the first will be exalted by God (see 1 Pet 5:6; Jas 4:10); what awaits those who seek the second is deception (Matt 24:24) or worse (Matt 7:22–23; Acts 8:19). Nevertheless, many Christians today understand the realization of the miraculous event as the determining sign of true faith and spirituality in the believer: "If you *really* believe, you will see the extraordinary happen from the hand of God! If you are not experiencing such manifest power in your life, it is no doubt because you are not spiritual enough—that is, your faith is too weak!" To *stand by* the view that the miraculous is indeed the end-all of Christian faith requires that you *stand on* the assumption that God's supreme desire for his church is that the community of believers experience manifestations of the supernatural, for that which God designates as the main objective of faith is what God wills for his people to possess above all else.

Pneumatolatry

The case I have been building is this: whatever the Lord desires we obtain through asking, we *do* obtain by asking because the Lord wants us to obtain it, having promised and guaranteed it through our asking for it. The question remains, however, as to why so many believers fail to obtain convincingly or satisfactorily their own "personal Pentecostal existence," though they seek it continuously with all their hearts.

It cannot be because they have no faith at all, because the very fact that they ask God demonstrates that they do indeed believe God has promised to give what they pray for. Otherwise, why ask him? The problem could be that their faith is vacillating or unsure and that they do not ask from a center of total dependence on God—that is, they have "little faith."[21] In practice, however, this would mean that many suffer from an extremely debilitating faith, one that shows little or no growth throughout their lives, for many, most, or arguably *all* who seek the precise experiences of the first Christians go to their graves falling short of their goal. Yet Jesus said all that is needed to move a mountain is faith the size of a mustard seed (cf. Matt 17:19–20).

I do not mean to be flippant here; the stakes are too high. To pray for a lifetime for what God explicitly promised to give us through asking without ever receiving it reflects poorly on God, who himself works in us sufficiently (2 Cor 3:5) to will and to work for his good pleasure (Phil 2:12), equipping us with all we need to do his will (Heb 13:21). Is it possible that the Holy Spirit is incapable of working even an average faith in the children of God throughout the course of their lives so that they might receive what they ask for according to God's will? Or is it perhaps the case that God simply does not expect his church to be so driven in asking for certain things? I would submit that the problem is not lack of faith—a much abused and misused excuse—but a misunderstanding of what God wants us to be seeking in our praying.

James teaches that we do not receive if we do not ask, but also if we ask wrongly—that is, in order to satisfy our own passions (Jas 4:2–3). But there is another way to ask wrongly so as not to receive: if we turn to God to ask for things he has not promised as if he has. In pneumatolatry, both ways are present, either as the result of ignorance or arrogance. First, and without doubting the sincerity of many to see the glory of God in manifest power, there is a strong motivation in pneumatolatry to ask for manifestations of the Spirit to avoid being downgraded to a lower spiritual level.

---

21. See Osborne, *Matthew*, 601.

In experientialist circles, those who do not have personal testimonies of experiencing God's power in the form of signs, tongues, prophecies, exorcisms, healings, and miracles are often labeled as somehow less spiritual than those who have many personal stories of such experiences. Surely asking to experience God's power for this reason is a case of asking in order to spend it on our own passions or our own vanity. Second, and more to the point theologically, it is rampant within pneumatolatrous groups to ask for the Holy Spirit and things pertaining to his ministry that the Holy Spirit himself has never taught us to ask for.

Pray the Teaching, Not the Experience!

Assemblies of God scholar Glen W. Menzies' assessment of the early Pentecostals helps put into historical perspective where and how this asking for what was never promised by the Lord began in our contemporary context.[22] Concerning the fundamental difference between how the Reformers understood a return to New Testament Christianity and how the early Pentecostals understood it, Menzies writes:

> Had not the Protestant Reformation amounted to a similar claim? Had not Luther claimed that the Roman Church had become apostate and needed to be restored or reformed? Was not the Reformation slogan *Ad fonts*—"To the sources"—a cry for restoration to New Testament Christianity? But the early Pentecostals claimed more than the Reformers. They called for a restoration not only of apostolic doctrine, but also apostolic experience. They claimed that the same life and power that animated the Church during the Apostolic Age was once again present in their midst. They claimed it was possible to live the book of Acts in the twentieth century.[23]

This understanding of the will of God for the church is standard fare for Pentecostal and charismatic Christians till this day. What interests us here is how this belief has influenced the substance and direction of what it essentially means to be a spiritual Christian. Consequently, it has also given shape to a prayer life in many believers that, I argue, does not correspond to those of Christ and the apostles.

In the only place in the New Testament where we find an extended instruction on what the content of prayer should be, Jesus taught his

---

22. Menzies himself would likely dispute my application of his findings.
23. Menzies, "A Full Apostolic Gospel," 26.

Pneumatolatry

disciples to pray that the Father's will proceed unhindered in the cosmos, that the disciples receive their daily needs from heaven, that they might be forgiven even as they forgave, and that they be spared temptation and protected from evil (Matt 6:10–13). In short, the prayer was a request for the power and grace of God so that the church might "renounce ungodliness and worldly passions, and to live self-controlled, upright, and godly lives in the present age" as it waits for Christ to return (Titus 2:12–13). Paul prays for the Thessalonians that God might make them worthy of God's calling and, by his power, render them able to fulfill their every desire to do good and perform every act of faith (2 Thess 1:11). Similarly, Peter understood that God's mighty power was granted to us so that we might truly live in Christ-like godliness, for only in this way could we become partakers of the divine nature (2 Pet 1:3–4). Indeed the context in which Jesus taught his disciples how to pray was his most complete teaching on how to live powerful spiritual lives in the fear of the Lord (Matt 5–7). Thus, the attainment of a cross-centered life was to be the *fundamental* content of prayer that would procure the power and grace necessary to live in imitation of Christ and complete the mission he outlined in the great mandate passages of the gospels. And Jesus fully expected that whoever asked for such power would find the way to obtain it (Matt 7:8)!

Experientialist Christian prayer life today, however, often consists above all in asking for manifest and not veiled power. Paul took for granted that the congregation was to experience a deeply charismatic life.[24] But the significant shortage in the New Testament of explicit teaching on asking for certain phenomena indicates that Jesus and the apostles did not envision the desire for manifest power as dominating the minds and hearts of believers.[25] We certainly never find any indication that believers are to ask for heavenly manifestations of the Spirit simply in order to embellish their worship or make them feel good spiritually, though concrete demonstrations of God's manifest power in the assembly do accomplish these things. By far, the majority of biblical teaching on what to ask of God circles around (1) deliverance from that which opposes God's will, (2) grace and

---

24. See Turner, "Gifts of the Spirit."

25. The closest we come to finding instruction to pray specifically for the so-called charismatic or supernatural gifts is in 1 Cor 14:13 and Jas 5:16, where believers are exhorted to ask for the ability to interpret tongues and for healing, respectively. Both of these instances, however, are set in contexts of sanctification. I have discussed this briefly above when commenting on the "eagerly desire the greater gifts" passage.

power for godly living, and (3) the effective spread of the gospel, mainly through effective preaching.[26]

Contrary to what is commonly believed and taught, the baptism with the Holy Spirit in Luke's description of Pentecost does not point to a church that should expect a charismatic power-fest. Rather, it underscores mission and cross-centered discipleship. Concerning the purpose of Pentecost, Craig S. Keener writes,

> God poured out the Spirit to empower his people to evangelize cross-culturally, but what was the anticipated outcome of cross-cultural evangelism? God intended to create a new community in which believers would love one another and demonstrate to this age the very image of the life of his kingdom.[27]

In a similar vein, there are no scriptural instances in which Christ fills believers with his Spirit for the sake of the experience alone. When the disciples do ask to be glorified on one occasion (apparently for the sake of it), Jesus corrects them, for they had yet to understand that what they had asked for required a deep work of the cross in their lives. Predictably, a divisive spirit ensued (Mark 10:35–41), for seeking glory and power without understanding the role the cross must play in our lives inevitably leads to presumption and contention. Not even Jesus' final priestly prayer for his disciples involves asking that they might do the miracles he had done; rather, he asks that they might by united to and in God (John 17:11), kept from the evil one (John 17:15), be sanctified in the truth (John 17:17), and be with him with the Father (John 17:24).

From this survey, it would appear that asking for a baptism or filling of the Holy Spirit, if it is to be heeded by God, must come from the mouths of those eager to announce the cross of Christ and be themselves humbled by it and not for the sake of speaking in tongues, prophesying, casting out demons, or performing signs and wonders. What the Spirit of God does subsequently is up to him.

For even when the disciples asked the Lord in prayer to stretch out his hand to heal and do signs and wonders, it was clearly subordinate to their desire to announce the gospel with boldness, which, by the way, God honored (Acts 4:29–31). And even where Paul exhorts the Corinthian believers

---

26. Matt 5:44; 9ff.; 9:38; 18:19; 24:20; 26:41, and parallel; Luke 18:1; Acts 8:22; 2 Cor 9:14; 13:7, 9; Col 1:3–4, 9; 4:3; 1 Thess 3:10; 5:16–18, 25; 2 Thess 1:11; 3:1; 1 Tim 2:8; Phlm 1:6; Heb 13:18; Jas 1:5; 5:16; 1 John 5:16; 3 John 1:2; Jude 1:20.

27. Keener, "Power of Pentecost," 70.

to seek the gifts, he stresses prophecy and not tongues because it is, simply put, greater insofar as it produces an intelligible proclamation of the gospel and is therefore useful for the "upbuilding and encouragement and consolation" of the entire body (1 Cor 14:1–5). It is to *this* greatness that the Christian life is to be directed.

My argument, therefore, is not an anti-charismatic alarmist rant—far from it, for I believe God's will is that the church worship together in full exercise of kingdom power. My criticism, rather, is aimed at an idolatry of the heart that plays around with God's priorities such that the *charismata* replace the cross as the basis and goal of Christian spirituality and the pursuit of the spectacular substitutes the quest for godliness. I would submit that it matters little whether pneumatolaters are often zealous evangelists, because as long as they announce the gifts over the cross—or even as somehow coequal with it—they are preaching another gospel.

Pneumatolatry can be traced back to the original Pentecostal agenda Menzies indicated above. The conviction that today we are able to relive the identical charismatic experience of the apostolic church gives rise to a belief system that produces requests other than those actually taught by Christ and the apostles. For this reason, so much of early Pentecostal and charismatic doctrine has had to undergo revision within their own circles (see chapter 1). Such doctrine has had to be reworked because it tried fitting the teaching of Jesus and the apostles into a theology shaped not by their doctrine but by their experiences of manifest power. "While the early Pentecostals valued deep devotion and piety,"[28] the thrust of the movement from the beginning was to live out a reproduced apostolic charismatic experience. Since they claimed it was possible to live the book of Acts in their contemporary setting, it was only natural that their prayer life should move out from under the shadow of the cross and into the perceived sunshine of the miraculous and extraordinary. As a result, generation after generation has been taught to ask above all for the latter.

It may be said without exaggeration, I think, that many today are more concerned with asking for what Jesus and the apostles experienced than with what they actually taught us to ask for. This is crucial, of course, and brings us face to face with the previous point concerning worship: the follower of Christ must take the utmost care not to deviate from the Lord's precise instructions. The proviso that new disciples were to be instructed to observe *all* that Jesus had taught—and not what he had experienced—was,

---

28. Menzies, "A Full Apostolic Gospel," 26.

after all, part of Jesus' great mandate (Matt 28:20). Those who might object by affirming the need to "let the Spirit out of the box" forget that it was the Spirit who inspired the "box" in the first place. Furthermore, with just the slightest adjustment, this slogan becomes "Don't be so slavishly beholden to walk the narrow path; have the courage to take excursions every now and then."

There is of course a danger if we conceive of the "narrow path" more narrowly than Jesus did. It is quite clear that this path should be broad enough to host the full range of charismata. It is open enough to celebrate the experiences of the supernatural that God does give and to let our "religiously correct" guard down in the full joy of the Spirit. The Lord appears to have fewer problems with food, drink, and merrymaking than many Christians do (see Ecclesiastes), as long as our celebrations are done in the fear of the Lord under the shadow of the cross. For if the cross is active in our lives, and if we are vigilant, we need not fear excesses—we *can* let go and fully trust the Holy Spirit because the cross keeps bringing us back . . . well, to the cross! It is our built-in safety protector. The problem only arises when we let go while not living under the power of Calvary—when we stop seeking Christ's cross in perusal of his particular experiences.

EMBODYING SPIRITUALITY IN IMITATION OF CHRIST

> Be imitators of me, as I am of Christ. (1 Cor 11:1)

As we examine Scripture, we find no teaching that any one generation of God's people should actively seek the experiences of a previous generation. Joshua was never commanded to chase after Moses' experiences of God even though he was promised that the Lord would be with him even as he had been with Moses. While not lacking by any means the extraordinary works of God in his life, Joshua's experiences were slightly less "spectacular" overall than his predecessor's was. In terms of moral stature, faithfulness, and importance, Samuel would appear to have been superior to the judges that preceded him. Like them, he too had the Spirit of the Lord upon him, but he never knew, nor was he commanded by the Lord to seek the extraordinary experiences of Othniel, Gideon, Jephthah, and Samson. The Spirit was clearly upon the writing prophets, and their value to God's plan of redemption is incalculable, yet we never read of them as performing or

Pneumatolatry

asking for the miraculous power of Elijah and Elisha.[29] Paul never instructs his prize pupil Timothy to imitate him by seeking to ascend into the third heaven, raise the dead, or heal the sick by his handkerchiefs and aprons (Acts 19:12). Rather, he exhorts him to follow the pattern of the sound words he had heard from him, "in the faith and love that are in Christ Jesus" (2 Tim 1:13). Likewise, while the writer of Hebrews reminds his readers of how God bore witness to the gospel they first heard by many miraculous works and signs (Heb 2:4), he never instructs that they should therefore also seek such things. Rather, he exhorts them to consider the lives of their godly elders and to imitate their faith (Heb 13:7).[30] For the writer knew that tasting the powers of the age to come was no guarantee of salvation (Heb 6:4–6). Those who persevered in cross-shaped faith producing holiness, however, would "see the Lord" (Heb 12:14).

In the same vein, there is neither teaching nor even any suggestion that successive generations of the church should actively seek to replicate the precise experiences of the church in Acts.[31] Certainly, the further away we move from New Testament times, the greater the difficulty in comprehending with precision what the early church experienced. Concerning the attempt to relive the experience of the Corinthian church, Raymond Brown writes, "No person reared in the twentieth century has the worldview of a person reared in the first century, and therefore it is impossible today to know or duplicate exactly what Paul describes, no matter how genuine the self-assurance of the charismatic."[32]

---

29. It is commonly mistaken that Elisha asks for Elijah's ability to perform great acts. He asks instead for his spirit (Heb. *ruach*), which clearly refers to the *prophetic* "fire" burning in him to obey the Lord. Surely, the writing prophets had the same spirit, though without the divine license to perform precisely the same miraculous works.

30. Interestingly, it is in this context of imitating the *holiness* of those who came before that we find another misused proof text supposedly demonstrating that we are to seek the signs and wonders performed by the apostles—namely, because "Jesus Christ is the same yesterday and today and forever" (Heb 13:8).

31. When Jesus says that anyone who believes in him will do "greater works" than those he did (John 14:12), Leon Morris is right that the Lord was referring to the day of Pentecost and beyond. But he is also probably right when he states that in the narrative of Acts we see a few miracles of healing but many conversions through the preaching of the gospel, so the "greater works" Jesus had in mind in reference to the outpouring of the Holy Spirit were those of conversion and not of miracles (Morris, *Gospel According to John*, 573–74). While this interpretation does not exclude greater miraculous works, the burden of proof lies with those who claim that here Jesus was referring to miracles rather than to conversions.

32. Brown, *Introduction to the New Testament*, 532. While Brown is correct from a

Indeed, it appears that the later New Testament church was already beginning to pass on from the early Acts experience to a post-apostolic reality. It continued in the teachings and deeds of Christ, but it would seem with a diminishing intensity of the miraculous.[33] In Heb 2:4, for example, the writer's argument is that his second-generation Christian readers could surely trust the gospel they had received, because its announcement had been accompanied by supernatural "signs and wonders and various miracles and by the gifts of the Holy Spirit distributed according to his will." However, there is no indication that the author supposes these signs and wonders to be normative for his readers; it simply is not his point. On the contrary, the force of his argument rests on the fact that such things happened at the specific time of the original *ingress* of the new covenant message in their midst, serving as a sort of "heavenly apologetic" for those (most probably Jews) who would have expected that the climactic event ushering in the new covenant would be assisted by prodigious signs and wonders that recalled God's actions during the inauguration of the first covenant.[34]

As already stated, the miraculous was central to Jesus and the apostles' life but not to their teaching. The "way" they taught had to do above all with the passing of human beings from darkness into light. That is to say, they taught a salvation that began with the knowledge of God's gracious

---

purely historical, institutional perspective, I have argued elsewhere that the regenerate Christian of any age remains profoundly united to the first-century church *mystically*. This creates a tension. From the cultural-historical side, each successive generation of the church moves farther away from the New Testament reality. From the mystical, the regenerate church of any age remains ever near the church of the apostolic age. Nevertheless, this does not overturn Brown's fundamental insight. See Zito, "Mystical Union as Interpretive Community," esp., 226–66.

33. That the ultra-charismatic character of the first decades of the church was already waning is the working theory in Kim, "Johannine Root of Pentecostalism." In this article, Kim maintains that the Johannine writings served as a corrective criticism of a church that was already becoming more and more institutionalized, rationalistic, and in need of rebuke in order to return to its true charismatic identity. I would affirm that the decline of the miraculous is biblically defensible, but that Kim's thesis suffers from a skewed methodology that tends to interpret the Johannine literature charismatically (or mystically) on the basis of the somewhat enigmatic writing style employed. On the contrary, these writings are much more concerned with correct doctrine and practice ("truth," "light," "life," "the way," "seducers," etc.) than with the church's charismatic identity.

34. We need to be careful here because different from the mosaic covenant, the new covenant established the coming of the kingdom of God on earth, which is characterized by heavenly power poured out on all who belong to Christ. See below.

forgiveness followed by a spiritual-ethical formation of Christ in the believer unto a life of faithful service. While Jesus and the apostles certainly expected the believer to be filled with the same power of the Holy Spirit they had known and to experience the outworking of the kingdom, they never alluded in their teaching to the need for Christians to be empowered to perform the same signs and wonders they did. The claim that the Bible clearly teaches that succeeding generations of believers are to relive the book of Acts simply cannot be sustained without interpreting Scripture according to one of the most basic hermeneutical fallacies—namely, that "what happened" in the past is *ipso facto* what is to be expected in the present. As a literary genre, narratives recount what was; they are descriptive, not prescriptive.

Yet disciples are prescribed to imitate Christ and, secondarily, the apostles, their church elders, and any godly man or woman. What, therefore, are we to imitate? An examination of the "imitation" (*mimetes/mimeomai*) passages in the New Testament is revealing. The majority of texts containing either the words or concepts of "imitation," "example," "follow," and the like concerning Jesus and the apostles have to do with reproducing their spiritual-ethical-ministerial character.[35] This is simply another way of saying that "the language of imitation is closely associated with the cross . . . the sign under which all Christian life this side of the *Parousia* is judged."[36] Not one of them even intimates that the disciple should imitate the supernatural works of Christ or Paul, because no one will be judged over such matters. Rather than pointing to the life of the genuine disciple, "signs and wonders" passages usually serve to either warn believers of false prophets[37] or speak of those who needed signs because of little faith.[38]

Where signs and wonders are seen in a positive light, they usually "indicate those miraculous acts associated with the outpouring of the Spirit in 'the last days' that God does to attest his messengers."[39] Such statements,

---

35. See John 1:11; Rom 15:12; 1 Cor 4:16; 11:1; Eph 5:1; Phil 2:5; 3:17; 1 Thess 1:6; 2:14; 2 Thess 3:7, 9; Heb 6:12; 13:7. This is even true of the "follow me" passages in the Gospel of John that many understand in terms of a call into his miraculous ministry through belief in him. While Jesus does call people to follow him from the world into the kingdom, his notion of belief or faith is never void of the idea of total faithfulness to the way of the cross. See, for example, John 10:4–5, 27; 12:26; 13:36; 21:19; 22.

36. Fowl, "Imitation of Paul/of Christ."

37. See Matt 24:24; 13:22; 2 Thess 2:9; cf. Mark 16:17.

38. See John 4:48; 6:2ff; 12:37; 1 Cor 1:22.

39. Davids, "Signs and Wonders."

however, must be supplemented by a more integral understanding of the attestation of God's kingdom: "For Luke, Jesus' miracles do not illustrate or demonstrate the good news; they are themselves (with his teaching) the good news"[40] (Luke 11:20). To put it another way, for Jesus, the signs and wonders are "expressions of the liberating reign of God, bursting into history, and it is *as such* that they attest the message of the kingdom."[41] While the truths expressed in these statements point to a much more dynamic kingdom in post-apostolic times than many are willing to admit, it still does not require us to assert that the signs and wonders performed at the inauguration of the kingdom by Jesus and the apostles are to be sought after or even expected in imitation by successive generations of Christians.

Nevertheless, it is commonly argued that since the "last days" were inaugurated with the coming of the kingdom and again powerfully at Pentecost, then all that follows must follow the same paradigm to the letter. Thus, even contemporary bearers of the gospel should expect God to confirm their communication of the gospel through signs and wonders as well. It seems to me that the biblical evidence points to a more restrictive use of such attestations, referring *in particular* to the apostolic period surrounding Pentecost without closing the door to such happenings in the future.

This can be verified through a number of biblical reflections. First, it is shown by the mere number of times that the signs and wonders performed by Jesus, the apostles, or their close associates are specifically claimed to be substantiations of the inauguration of the kingdom and the once-and-for-all stamp of approval on both its message and its messengers.[42] Jesus cogently reinforces the idea that signs and wonders play an important but limited role in redemptive history and that the message is effective on its own. He teaches explicitly, in fact, that supernatural evidences have little to no power to change a hardened heart. The Scripture is sufficient for the job. If people do not heed the gospel message as it is announced, not even a resurrection in their midst can lead them to repentance (Luke 16:29–31). Indeed, as Jesus teaches, "Blessed are those who have not seen and yet believed" (John 20:29). Faith comes from hearing through the word of Christ (Rom 10:17) and not from seeing through miracles; it is the conviction of

---

40. Twelftree, "Signs and Wonders."
41. Turner, "Gifts of the Spirit."
42. Acts 5:12; 6:8; 8:6, 13; 14:3; 15:12 (this passage seems to indicate that signs and wonders were not the norm but were instead special events); 19:11; Rom 15:19; 2 Cor 12:12; Heb 2:4; Rev 13:13–14; 16:14; 19:20.

Pneumatolatry

things heard but not seen (Heb 11:1). Furthermore, John the Evangelist informs us that he has written down a portion of the signs Jesus did so that through *reading* (or hearing) about them, his audience might believe and have life in his name (John 20:31). Concerning the signs of Jesus, John points us back, not forward.

In God's plan, faith comes from hearing and not from seeing, though it was divinely established that in order for the authoritative bearers of the once-and-for-all gospel to be believed, they should be authenticated through signs and wonders. To the assertion that we need to ask that these signs might happen in our midst in order to glorify God, I would reply that a miracle, a healing, or a supernatural wonder in the Spirit's hands does indeed bring glory to God, but by God's own standards it is a lesser glory than the power of the cross bringing about repentance or the consequent harvest of peace and righteousness through proclamation of and faith in the gospel (John 12:24). Jesus was aware that his miraculous deeds glorified the Father; he also understood that the miracles were an inferior way of doing so. For whenever he spoke of himself and his Father being glorified through him—that is, glorified inclusively, once and for all within the redemptive scheme—it was always by means of the cross rather than through any sign or wonder.[43] In imitation of Christ, the disciple glorifies God through the cross transforming a selfish, unloving child of darkness into a person who lives to serve God and others[44] and in announcing God's mercy in saving the lost.[45] For this reason, the Lord never asked his disciples to pray for power to perform miracles or for the experience of signs and wonders but rather for the strength to live a godly, fruit-bearing life made possible by the cross.

Indeed, this is usually how the apostles themselves prayed for the churches:

> To this end we always pray for you, that our God may make you worthy of his calling and may fulfill every resolve for good and every work of faith by his power, so that the name of our Lord Jesus may be glorified in you, and you in him, according to the grace of our God and the Lord Jesus Christ. (2 Thess 1:11–12)

To teach believers that they are not to expect the miraculous from God is patently erroneous. Those who, through the cross, die to self in order to

---

43. See John 8:54; 12:28; 13:31–32; 17:1, 5; 21:19; Acts 3:13; Rom 15:8–9.
44. See Rom 8:17; 1 Cor 6:20; 2 Cor 9:13; 1 Pet 2:12; 4: 11, 16.
45. See Acts 11:17; 21:20; Gal 1:24.

walk in the fullness of Christ's Spirit will be in harmony with what God is doing at any one time in the church and in the world. Just as God can and does do abundantly more than what we ask or think of according to the power that works in us (Eph 3:20), he will do greater things than we expect. However, the teaching that believers are to actively seek the supernatural experiences of Jesus and the apostles cannot be justified by Scripture and plays into the hands of Satan in at least two ways. First, it is a distraction from seeking what Jesus and the apostles actually taught us to pursue. Second, it opens the door for the fleshliest kind of Christianity because it comes to perceive the way of the cross as too inhibitive and a deterrent to the "true" spirituality of glory, signs, and wonders that the cross of Jesus delivered to the church. It is halfway to another gospel.

CONCLUDING THOUGHTS

In this section, I addressed a number of errors committed by experientialist Christianity. Primarily, it holds in light regard how the Holy Spirit has revealed God, including the Spirit's own Person, through the Scriptures. This levity concerning revealed truth leads to all the other errors. The fundamental mistake is to allow experiences—both personal and those of others—to dictate what is true about the Holy Spirit. Rather than bringing a balance to a rationalistic spirituality through integrating experience into a general hermeneutic of the Bible,[46] this mistake obscures the explicit teaching of Jesus and the apostles by insisting that their experiences are as normative as their instruction for the Christian life.

What ensues is a wrong picture of what it is to be united to God in the kingdom—i.e., what it is to be spiritual. This view centers on the miraculous and the extraordinary. The more God's wonders abound, the deeper the experience of unity with God becomes. In practice, this premise inevitably creates a spiritual mind-set and vocabulary that tends to shun the language of the cross in favor of what we might call "glory-speak." It underestimates and even avoids the cross as the preferred medium of power and glory in God's kingdom and substitutes it for an idealized version of the experience of the church as portrayed in Acts. It takes lightly the Scripture's (including Acts') own finely tuned explanations for the signs and wonders within the divine redemptive scheme, substituting them instead with interpretations

---

46. I attempt to lay a theological groundwork for such a hermeneutic in Zito, "Mystical Union."

Pneumatolatry

of personal charismatic experiences. Surely, to jump from an outbreak of early twentieth-century, like-minded American evangelicals speaking in strange tongues to a dogma that God had re-endowed the contemporary church with a second Pentecost betrays both an overconfident spirit and a superficial understanding of the subtleties of redemptive history. To turn Pentecost into a miracle-fest is childish at best, presumptuous and wrong-headed at worst. It moves beyond an over-realized eschatology to an *inflated* eschatology. What the church seeks and asks for above all else as God's design for the Holy Spirit is, in fact, off target. Paul put it most succinctly: "[T]his is the will of God, your sanctification" (1 Thess 4:3a). A little later, he finished his thought:

> For God has not called us for impurity, but in holiness. Therefore whoever disregards this, disregards not man but God, who gives his Holy Spirit to you. (1 Thess 4:7–8)

Of course, sanctification and supernatural deeds are not mutually exclusive. As I have insisted throughout this chapter, God can and still does work miracles, do wonders, heal, and the like. The risen Christ is still the compassionate Christ of the gospels, and the Holy Spirit is still the dispenser of all kinds of gifts. Real faith does get answers, even of God's manifest power. Yet Christ's greatest act of compassion and the Spirit's greatest gift of all are to save people out of a lost, miserable, and sinful existence and place them into his kingdom of light to walk in it. The supreme power of Christ—his *true* life of love and faithfulness leading to and then beyond the cross to resurrection—is the light of the kingdom (John 1:4). Yes, there is power available for mighty deeds, but to think that these are God's end game, to believe that without experiencing them we are undone and unspiritual, reveals a misguided understanding of spirituality.

To know God in fellowship with God is to be submitted to the way of the cross, for only in dying to ourselves are we able to live unto Christ. The Apostle Paul, perhaps more gifted and blessed than any man outside of of the Lord Jesus—he who raised the dead, came back from the near-dead, healed the sick, performed miracles, was prophesied over, and taken up into the third heaven—never considered such things as the content of true spirituality. For him, true spirituality—being in the right kind of positional and practical relationship with God—was a matter of the cross of Christ doing its work in his life so that he could better serve the Lord and live for him and others with the time he had been given on earth.

DOCTRINE AND EXPERIENCE

I shall end with this striking passage by Paul full of references to true spirituality (as I have conceived it)—that is, knowledge of God that unites us to God in Christ's love and through the Holy Spirit's power:

> But whatever gain I had, I counted as loss for the sake of Christ. Indeed, I count everything as loss because of the surpassing worth of knowing Christ Jesus my Lord. For his sake I have suffered the loss of all things and count them as rubbish, in order that I may gain Christ and be found in him, not having a righteousness of my own that comes from the law, but that which comes through faith in Christ, the righteousness from God that depends on faith—that I may know him and the power of his resurrection, and may share his sufferings, becoming like him in his death, that by any means possible I may attain the resurrection from the dead. Not that I have already obtained this or am already perfect, but I press on to make it my own, because Christ Jesus has made me his own. Brothers, I do not consider that I have made it my own. But one thing I do: forgetting what lies behind and straining forward to what lies ahead, I press on toward the goal for the prize of the upward call of God in Christ Jesus. Let those of us who are mature think this way, and if in anything you think otherwise, God will reveal that also to you. Only let us hold true to what we have attained. Brothers, join in imitating me, and keep your eyes on those who walk according to the example you have in us. For many, of whom I have often told you and now tell you even with tears, walk as enemies of the cross of Christ. Their end is destruction, their god is their belly, and their glory in their shame, with minds set on earthly things. But our citizenship is in heaven, and from it we await a Savior, the Lord Jesus Christ, who will transform our lowly body to be like his glorious body, by the power that enables him even to subject all things to himself. (Phil 3:7–21)

Chapter 4

Spirituality Caught in the Crossfire of Doctrine and Experience

> At times an individual may think that she has arrived at a clear understanding of Christian spirituality only to discover that a new experience, or perhaps the reflection on another person's experience, calls into question what was first believed and the conversation between belief and experience is held again. To put it another way, just when a person feels at home with a particular doctrine, experience may tap on the door of belief or vice versa and the conversation between doctrine and experience begins again.[1]

INTRODUCTION

Summary Thus Far, Thesis, and Method

At the beginning of this book, I gave a provisory definition of spirituality as that knowledge of the divine that connects us to the divine. I went on from there to describe evangelical spirituality as that knowledge of God that unites us to God in a personal, saving relationship in accordance with the gospel. In the second and third chapters, I examined, compared, and contrasted respectively a doctrinally-based spirituality and an experiential-

---

1. Smith, *Christian Spirituality*, 10–11.

ly-based one as they have taken shape in contemporary evangelicalism (at least in the West). Doctrinalist spirituality affirms that the knowledge of God that unites us to him is derived from comprehending and then assenting to right statements about God as revealed in the Bible. Experientialists argue that true spirituality derives primarily from the experience one has of God, who reveals himself above all through the manifestation(s) of the Holy Spirit.[2] I criticized both models for being reductionistic and failing to integrate adequately the other's concerns within their own belief systems.

Within the thematic arc of the third chapter, a different dialectic emerged, this time between what we might call a *spirituality of the cross* and a *spirituality of glory*.[3] With the first, I affirmed that true spirituality is the result of the veiled power of the cross at work in the believer's life, causing us to die to self in order to live unto God. With the second, I alluded disapprovingly to a Christian worldview that perceives the miraculous or otherwise extraordinary—what I termed the manifest power of God—as the building blocks of true spirituality.

In this chapter, I will move beyond this crossroads towards what I consider a more fully-orbed evangelical spirituality. Ideally, such spirituality avoids the excesses of both doctrinalism and experientialism, while at the same time taking seriously the interests of both. I realize that this last statement may seem incongruous, as I have just identified the practices and theologies of bibliolaters and pneumatolaters alike as touching on idolatrous. However, I never conceived of my criticisms as instruments for

---

2. Cf. Donald Bloesch's notions of Logos and Spirit Christolgies in Bloesch, *Holy Spirit*, 222–23.

3. This recalls Luther's famous distinction in the *Heidelberg Theses* (1815) between *theologia crucis* and *theologia gloriae*, by which he contrasts two concurrent approaches to the knowledge of God. For Luther, the cross is the foundation and center of all theology in that it is the focal point of God's revelation of himself (and thus of true knowledge). My understanding of spirituality as cross-centered is definitely in line with Luther's theology of the cross. My spirituality of glory, however, takes a different track than his theology of glory. Luther understands the theology of glory in a medieval, scholastic context that elevated natural theology—God's goodness, power, and glory as manifested in the works of creation—to an unjustifiably prominent position. See Bauckham, "Theology of the Cross." My use of a theology of glory is tied instead to our contemporary context, in which the manifest power of God substitutes the work of the cross in the believer's life as the basis of true spirituality. This, in turn, leads to what Saint John of the Cross referred to as spiritual gluttony, which is characterized by striving after "spiritual sweetness" (read: "experiences") more than by spiritual purity and discretion, as well as the belief that this is the path established by God for those seeking true spirituality (Saint John of the Cross, *Dark Night of the Soul*, I.VI).

mocking the importance of either doctrine or experience for a Christian spirituality but simply as warnings against the reductionistic reliance on either to the exclusion of the other.

I will now argue that both aspects are essential to a robust evangelical spirituality. As our historical survey showed, the debate between doctrinalism and experientialism has shaped the entire history of Protestantism up until our present day. In reality, the conflict goes back to the beginnings of the church. Rarely has a single movement or group been able to sustain a happy balance between doctrine and experience. Such movements are like flashing lights on the big screen of church history, intermittent phases in which doctrine and experience seemed to have been incorporated into a vital, thriving, Christian spirituality. In this chapter, I attempt to make some helpful considerations for forging a more balanced evangelical spirituality in the midst of a generation that is no less controversial, contentious, or partisan than any that came before.

My thesis is the following: true spirituality can only result when doctrine and experience are integrated correctly and vitally in the life of the church by a faith-based openness to the operations of the Holy Spirit in the forging of a cross-centered culture of fellowship as shown and taught in the Bible. The prosperity of the church in our time depends on having and living a right relationship between doctrine and experience in the light of Scripture and the Holy Spirit.

In order to test my thesis, I start with some systematic reflections on spirituality, methodically narrowing down my focus until I get to what the Bible has to say on the matter. I realize that this approach might seem like putting the cart before the horse and is, in fact, contrary to the order theologians usually employ. Nevertheless, I have worked in this way for the sake of clarity. The question of what actually constitutes spirituality today is a subject so vast and complex that it is nearly impossible to look at the biblical data without imposing on it an unwarranted quantity of preconceptions. After having brought some clarity to the discussion of spirituality as a whole, I then proceed to re-examine some relevant Scriptures. My aim is nothing so ambitions as starting a completely new line of inquiry, however. Rather, I work in this way to simply to re-examine what Scripture says about spirituality from the perspective of the contemporary doctrine/experience debate.

DOCTRINE AND EXPERIENCE

The Problem of Delineating Evangelical Spirituality

Bernard McGinn, the renowned Catholic historian of the mystical and spiritual tradition of the church, sums up the problem of spirituality studies today by arguing that in practice it is impossible to define the term "spirituality," even if we are able to recognize it when we see it. What McGinn wants to put across is that despite endless investigations and debates, the concept of spirituality remains largely in the eye of the beholder. Everyone seems to speak of spirituality, although at cross-purposes. This last point is demonstrable by the evolution of the use of the term "spiritual" in contemporary culture and in how it has crossed the threshold of religious discourse into secular jargon. To be sure, it has so deeply infiltrated secular consciousness that McGinn can wryly admit that he is waiting for "the moment (perhaps not far off) when a product will be advertised on national television because of the contribution it makes to some form of spirituality."[4]

However, it is not only in the broader field of the study of spirituality that we find difficulties of definition. Even in the narrower field of evangelical spirituality, we find a series of problems that, if possible, must be overcome. In a paper presented at the Evangelical Theological Society in 2001, Donald Whitney affirmed that since the Reformation, evangelicals have had difficulty delineating the limits of their spirituality because "the borders of Evangelical spirituality have always been subject to invasion by non-Evangelical forces."[5] Inherent in this statement is a basic problem: evangelicals struggle to have a spirituality that is particularly their own. Perhaps a major reason for this is that evangelicalism was born, at least in part, as a protest to spirituality.

As one scholar maintains, the Reformation was largely a reaction against a medieval mysticism that (1) elevated humanity to the level of the divine, thereby greatly diminishing the role of the grace of God for humanity; (2) was an expression of piety that ignored or denied the basic principles of the Reformation; and (3) was a religion of feeling that ignored the historical nature of Jesus Christ, which isolated the mystic in a prayer closet and divorced the activities of Christian faith from service.[6] Consequently, the Reformation aligned itself with a concept of Christianity that was dis-

---

4. McGinn, "Letter and the Spirit," 13. I pick up this strand of thought again in the next section.

5. Whitney, "Defining the Boundaries."

6. Foss, "Rethinking the Mystical," 148.

tinctly historical and with a literal interpretation of the Bible as opposed to the philosophical spirituality derived from medieval mysticism.

These historical conditions created a strong skepticism in the evangelical subconscious towards not only mysticism, but also spirituality in general. With the rise of successive Protestant scholastic movements (see chapter 1), this suspicion often (but not always) hardened into more and more literalist and rationalist approaches to the Bible and, consequently, to the faith itself. In this skepticism, there was increasingly less room for experience as an integral aspect of spirituality. Today neo-puritianism and neo-pietism are on the rise, and both attempt to integrate experience into their evangelical cultures. The former is very strong on doctrine, while the latter is far less so.

SPIRITUALITY IN THE CHURCH AND BEYOND

In the Church . . .

Over the centuries, the concept of spirituality has radically changed from what it originally meant in the New Testament. It originated in the Judeo-Christian faith, and, in a strict sense, it should not be applicable to unregenerate people, although nowadays it often is. The word "spiritual" entered the English language through the Latin term *spiritualis*, which is the translation of the Greek word *pneumatikos* in the New Testament. The word was a neologism perhaps coined by the Apostle Paul that simply meant "that which pertained to the Holy Spirit of God."[7] This was how it was understood by the apostolic and patristic fathers. Jerome made use of the adjective *spiritualis* as many as twenty-two times in his Vulgate translation of the Bible in the fourth and fifth centuries. The noun *spiritualitatis* ("spirituality") appeared for the first time a little later in the fifth century. From its entrance into the Latin language and spanning the entire period of the early Middle Ages, the term retained its New Testament sense of acting according to the Spirit of Jesus.[8]

In these same centuries, however, a number of cultural considerations were already influencing the notion of spirituality. In the West, people such as Tertullian, Ambrose, Jerome, and Augustine began conceiving of spirituality as something *contrary to materiality*. This Neoplatonic influence

---

7. Schneiders, "Theology and Spirituality," 257.
8. McGinn, "Letter and the Spirit," 14.

is observable in the approval these theologians took towards celibacy and other generally ascetic practices aimed at subduing the body and its passions.[9]

Another relevant example of the Neoplatonic influence—this time coming out of Eastern Christianity—was seen in the desert fathers of the fourth century. These monks, hermits, and anchorites abandoned the cities to live in the wild solitude of the various deserts in the Middle East. Lying behind this migration was a clear lack of confidence in the possibility of becoming truly spiritual in public surroundings. Closely tied to this separation from human culture was a radically changing view of spirituality. Rather than something achieved *through* the body, spirituality for the desert fathers came to be understood as the very act of *suppressing* the body.

While both the Western and Eastern churches moved away from a "spirituality of the body," neither conceived of it as attained through human effort but always and only as the gift of grace through the presence and the activity of the Holy Spirit.[10] It is generally accepted that in the twelfth century there was a critical particularization of the church's perception of spirituality. While the West was still employing *spiritualitatis* to refer to the work of the Holy Spirit in animating the Christian life, it came to be conceived by scholastic theologians as having to do with the soul *in contrast to* the body. From this point on, Western Christianity would perceive the material world—and especially the human body—as impediments to authentic spirituality.[11] This shift also manifested itself in another way. Starting from the thirteenth right through the sixteenth centuries, spirituality came to be considered as something that was also opposed to *temporality*. Consequently, the clergy of this period came to deem all their possessions and revenue—belonging as they did to the heavenly and not the earthly realms—as constitutive of that which was truly "spiritual." All that was outside the strictly ecclesial environment was seen as temporal and therefore unspiritual.

Once again in the seventeenth century, the meaning of "spirituality" assumed a more openly theological and practical tone, as it had in the early centuries of Christianity. Gone were the strictly philosophical and ecclesiastical connotations. But whereas in the early centuries of the church the theological notion of spirituality had to do with how the Holy Spirit

9. Collins, "What Is Spirituality?," 78.
10. See Schneiders, "Theology and Spirituality," 258.
11. McGinn, "Letter and the Spirit," 14.

produces works of faith, hope, and love in harmony with the instruction and lives of Jesus and the apostles, the term now came to refer strictly to the *inner life* and especially to the emotional aspect of our relationship with God.[12]

While this was a sort of revival of spirituality with respect to the immediately preceding centuries, the emphasis on the inner life caused excesses that remain with us until today. In France, Italy, and in Spain, for example, strong quietist and enthusiast movements arose. Condemned by Rome as heretical, *quietism* is a doctrine of Christian spirituality that elevates the passivity of the soul over and above human effort. Only once the soul is "quieted" can divine action truly prevail with the person. As a result, contemplation was replaced by meditation, vocal prayer by intellectual stillness, and pious human activity by passivity. *Enthusiasm*, on the other hand, promoted personal human experiences with God to the forefront of the faith. Consequently, the affective side of faith becomes of primary importance, because among all the human faculties, only feelings are able to directly express the result of the apprehension of God. The theological reason commonly given to justify such spirituality revolved around a notion of the Holy Spirit as more interested in the interior life than with the works of the body.

As a natural progression of the developments of the previous decades, the eighteenth century gave rise to a lively debate between those who believed that spirituality was only for a few Christians and those who claimed that all believers were called to this life. The debate arose in the first place, however, only because spirituality had by then become completely detached from the common works of the body and intimately tied to the fulfillment of the inner life. Consequently, spirituality came to be understood as referring to those of a more ascetic and mystical bent—i.e., those able to perfect the soul through spiritual exercises and the practice of the perfection of virtue.[13] In this, we see a modern version of medieval mysticism, far from the practical-ethical spirituality emphasized in Scripture.

Shifting the weight of spirituality away from the practical outworking of the Holy Spirit in the edification of the body of Christ to the experience of God in the individual soul through ascetic and contemplative exercises, the mystic became the religious flipside of the secular "alienated" modern man. In this process of privatization, spirituality turned into an individualism

12. Schneiders, "Theology and Spirituality," 259.
13. Ibid.

that is foreign not only to biblical but also to general culture, rooted as they both are in communal life.

While the biblical emphasis concerning practical spirituality is on the work of the Holy Spirit transforming the church into the image of Christ—body, soul, and spirit—the modern mystic stresses individuals' ability to improve their souls Christward. In fact, it was during this period that asceticism and mysticism became the actual content of spirituality. In this, we find the historical source for the widespread opinion today that spirituality has to do almost exclusively with the disposition or state of the inner person.

With this crisis in spirituality came opposition from the culture at large. No doubt, the condemnation of quietism by the Catholic Church played an important role in this hostility by marring public opinion to the point that in the eighteenth and nineteenth centuries both Catholics and Protestants felt the need to begin replacing the word "spirituality" with less offensive terms like "devotion" and "piety."[14] As the twentieth century approached, however, the term started making a comeback and even became fashionable. By the middle of last century, "spirituality" had fully taken root in the popular imagination, and since the 1970s it has made its influence felt worldwide.[15]

. . . And Beyond

The globalization of spirituality has been accomplished primarily by freeing spirituality from its exclusively Christian patrimony. In fact, nowadays almost every religion has its own "spirituality." An even more surprising and interesting development has to do with the adoption of the term by the non-religious and even anti-religious.[16] If, however, even the a-religious claim to be spiritual,[17] perhaps Gustavo Vinay is correct to claim that spirituality has indeed become a necessary pseudo-concept for which we cannot find a better substitute term.[18] The pessimism of Lucy Bregman is even

---

14. McGinn, "Letter and the Spirit," 14–15.
15. Ibid., 15.
16. Wiseman, *Spirituality and Mysticism*, 1.
17. See Schneiders, "Theology and Spirituality," 255. Schneiders identifies three non- or anti-religious spiritualities: feminist, black, and Marxist.
18. Vinay, "Spiritualità," 706.

more direct than Vinay's when she argues, "the quest for the true essential meaning of spirituality is a fool's errand."[19]

Despite the difficulties in defining the term, definitions continue to multiply. With a lengthy passage that is worth reproducing, Bregman tries to capture the paradoxical nature of the contemporary phenomenon:

> Who has not heard the term "spirituality" used recently, in contexts where its exact meaning is left deliberately open-ended, hard-to-pin-down, and obscure? Yet, whenever it is used, eyes light up, people respond with positive remarks about its importance, and we all feel better. "Spirituality" has become a "glow-word," such as "growth" and "process" and "relationship." It is a glow-word with some connection with religion, and to pastoral care. But why not just say "religion" or "pastoral care"? Why should "spirituality" have catapulted into such popularity and seemingly displaced these other terms? And, if we cannot define it once and for all, why have there been almost 100 attempts to do so by researchers, clinicians, therapists, and health professionals? Not to mention chaplains, pastors, and experts in "spirituality."[20]

In the attempt to give meaning to the current exuberant proliferation of the concepts of spirituality, Bregman cites three major progressions that have taken place in the recent past. First, "spirituality" has often come to replace "religion." This has happened in a contemporary postmodern context in which the public and all-encompassing nature of the historical religions is suspected as mere weapons of oppressive control. Second, the "new spirituality" has provided a private environment for the growing number of people who believe that religion is a strictly personal affair. In this case, "spirituality" is not seen as replacing "religion" understood in its historical dimensions but rather in its personal relational dimension with the transcendent. This notion of religion has been called by a number of names, three of which are "personal religion," "faith," and "invisible religion."[21]

The third and most important step "has been to move from a bi-polar or relational definition, toward one that is non-relational, and focuses solely on a 'spiritual core' or essence that defines our basic humanness."[22] With this, Bregman refers to a spirituality that, as the name suggests, has two

---

19. Bregman, "Defining Spirituality," 157.
20. Ibid.
21. Ibid.
22. Ibid., 157–58.

poles: the subjective and the objective. In traditional Christian spirituality, for example, the subjective side had to do with understanding, life, and choices of the believer. However, all this was meaningless without the objective pole, which is the triune God. According to the bipolar definition, spirituality requires both poles to be complete because it is based on a relationship between those who experience and what is experienced.[23]

Current definitions, however, have eliminated the objective side. This means that a person's spirituality is no longer situated in a relationship with someone or something that transcends itself. It is no longer a matter of some connection with Yahweh, Allah, the god Brahma, the Absolute Being, the universe, nature, or even other people. It consists instead in a relationship with the person's own essence or humanity—that is, with "Self." Now that "spirituality" has cut all ties with both the particular religions and with all social contexts, it has become little more than an expression of what people are saying about themselves. Thus, spirituality takes place entirely within the individual.[24]

In this development, we can observe the realization of the seventeenth century's shift in emphasis from the outer to the inner life. Originally, the change had occurred within a theological mysticism; currently, it has taken the shape of a psychological humanist mysticism by which individuals try to transcend themselves by digging deeper within their own being. The evolution has also been felt within evangelical spirituality, producing an inconsistency between a biblical view of humanity that has a prominent place for the physical body in spirituality versus a Neoplatonic anthropology that sees the body as inferior in importance to the immaterial aspect. This problem is felt within both doctrinalist and experientialist evangelicalism, though with important differences.

THE TURN TOWARDS THE INNER LIFE IN EVANGELICAL SPIRITUALITIES

How has the turn to the inner life affected evangelical experiential spirituality? As I have conceived it, the aim of experientialist spirituality is to encounter the presence of God in the believer's direct experience. The *modus operandi* to arrive at this encounter in much contemporary experientialism is to invoke the Holy Spirit—sometimes explicitly, sometimes

---

23. Ibid., 159.
24. Ibid., 165.

implicitly—by a communion of praise, worship, prayer, and, often, unknown tongues. While all of these practices are active and bodily, they are put into service for the purpose of creating a passive environment conducive to the reception of the Spirit in the soul.

Similarly to some of the spiritual exercises of the mystical tradition, the techniques used by pneumatolaters are effective for making the intellect increasingly idle as the affections rise in intensity. In this way, the worshipper is better positioned to accommodate the fleeting presence of God when it appears. The difference between classical mysticism and modern-day enthusiasm is that the latter does not practice its techniques in the solitude of the monastery cell but in the full fervor of a brash and uninhibited communal experience. It is not surprising, therefore, that the height of the experience of God in these environments is understood in terms of a communal reception of new revelations, touches of divine healing, prophecy, and the inner feeling of deep conviction and of joy or peace that surpass all understanding (see Phil 4:7). In these cases, participants are encouraged to "let go of their inhibitions," which is equivalent to the subjugation of the intellect and the will to the affective and unknown spheres. It is for this reason that experientialist meetings sometimes culminate in uncontrolled crying, laughing, or falling to the ground as well as a deep concern with interacting with the invisible world of angels and demons.

An implicit belief undergirding this approach is that the premeditated actions of the body (for example, singing, praise, the uplifting of the hands) serve a merely preparatory role for true spirituality, which is manifested only when the person is overwhelmed by the Spirit "from outside in." In this we can detect an odd mix of the methods and purposes of enthusiasm on the one hand and quietism on the other. That is to say, the involvement of strong feelings in the activities of the body creates a mood for passive experience of the presence of God. The moment of "contact" with the divine is often quite subdued, though powerful, but it subsequently flowers into a series of exuberant and systematically unrestrained "divine happenings." The constant throughout this process is the desire to free oneself from the perceived cultural, rational, religious, and even bodily restrictions imposed on us from without so we can enjoy a liberating, sanctified irrationality within that then bubbles back out to the community and the body. It is this kind of freedom that the experientialist believes is the work of the Holy Spirit when he is present in his fullness.

DOCTRINE AND EXPERIENCE

In a completely different but equally Neoplatonic way, the dualism of body and soul is also detectable in doctrinalist spirituality. In broad terms, the prevailing thought here is that the Holy Spirit does not manifest himself where biblical truth is not explicitly disclosed to the intellect. For this reason, it is rare to find in these environments unprompted "psalms, hymns and spiritual songs" (Col 3:16), shouts of joy or repentance, or the lifted hands and sprawled-out bodies understood as simple expressions of the believer's feeling in the presence of the Lord. What we find instead is an attitude of worship in which believers' spontaneity is actively mitigated by a robust interaction with biblical and theological content. In this way, rather than creating a free and joyful celebration of the whole person, the revelatory truth of God channels worship predominantly through the intellect and will. What could and should be a whole-hearted, joyful spontaneity in the exaltation of the person of Jesus Christ easily withers into a rational and volitional exercise of worshipping *concepts* of the risen Lord, often accompanied by deadening and forced repetition of superlatives applied to God. More often than not, the notions that are worshiped are determined by the denominational distinctions of the group in question.

Accordingly, this kind of spirituality yields prayers and praises that tend to be theologically and biblically erudite, even in situations that would appear to require openly emotional prayers. For example, it is interesting to note how difficult it is for doctrinalists to cry out to the Lord to heal someone by direct fiat. This is the case even when the sufferer is dear to the intercessor. Rather than hear candid and tearful entreaties for the afflicted, it is common to witness appeals laden with specifications that acknowledge God's sovereign right to *not* heal. While theologically accurate, such praying lacks the kind of unrestrained dependence on God that many biblical prayers display. Another practical example of how the outward manifestation of emotions or other kinds of enthusiasm are either clearly discouraged or silently frowned upon by doctrinalists is the almost universal aversion to bodily motion in communal worship. With some degree of credibility, conservative personality types can be seen as the reason for this restraint. However, the deeper motivation would appear to be a socially shared conviction that all human senses and faculties must be subordinate to reason and propriety.

As in the experientialist approach, doctrinalist spirituality also proves to be entrenched in a Neoplatonic dualism. The difference is that in doctrinalism, the interior aspect detached from the body is not the affections but the intellect. True doctrine is heralded as the center of spirituality because reason is implicitly understood as the image of God in humanity. Thus, in doctrinalism the intellect prevails over the body and all other faculties. What emerges is a "spirituality of mind" that marginalizes the rest of the human person, especially the body.

Interestingly, both experientialists and doctrinalists are known for their zeal concerning Christian activity, despite the Neoplatonic influences that would appear to necessitate a more passive spirituality. To the contrary, a criticism often launched from within each camp is that as evangelical Christians, they are *activists*, focusing so intently on "doing" that they neglect "being." The criticism itself, however, betrays a latent Neoplatonism, insofar as it dichotomizes "doing" as something that belongs to the body and "being" as belonging to the inner life. The two are regarded as independent of each other, with bodily activity viewed as the mere ethical fruit of our responsibility to God's commands, while the inner quality is the aspect that constitutes true spirituality.

AN EMBODIED SPIRITUALITY OF THE CROSS

Theological Considerations on Biblical Spirituality

Before examining the biblical data directly, it is worth briefly considering what I mean by the term "biblical spirituality." This is a theological task.

According to Sandra Schneiders, there are three possible ways we can understand the expression. First, it can refer to *the various spiritualities expressed in the Bible*.[25] What this view has going for it is that it appears the array of biblical characters did indeed seem to have lived out their relationship with God with disparate emphases. Schneiders also has a case—at least up to a point—when she suggests that the varied biblical phenomena legitimize the different spiritualities that we find in the history of the church and that at the same time warn against any insistence that only one of these should be exclusive.[26] The second way we can understand biblical spirituality, according to Schneiders, is as "*a pattern of Christian life* deeply imbued

---

25. Schneiders, "Biblical Spirituality," 134–35. For example, Schneiders writes of the deeply christocentric spirituality of Paul, John's contemplative spirituality centered on Jesus, the spirituality of the church in the pastoral epistles, and so on. One could argue, however, that rather than having a plurality of spiritualities, the Bible presents us with different shades of a single vision.

26. Ibid.

with the spirituality(ies) of the Bible." Thus, the term can refer to differing contemporary spiritualities that assume a biblical character, even if they are not all strictly biblical to the same degree.[27] A third possible way to define biblical spirituality is with reference to "*a transformative process of personal and communal engagement with the biblical text.*" Here Schneiders refers to a relationship with the Bible that transcends historical or literary studies—a reading of the Scriptures as the "word of God," as the living words spoken personally to us by the living God in the context of the community.[28]

All three of Schneiders' suggestions are attractive, in part because they avoid the mysticism of Neoplatonic spirituality. However, for the present purposes I prefer to interact with an approach like that of the evangelical theologian Donald Bloesch simply because it relates spirituality more directly to the biblical *content*. While Schneiders' models make ample room for the use of scriptural content, the definitions themselves tend to be hermeneutical in nature. On the other hand, Bloesch builds his understanding of spirituality directly on the biblical material and expounds it in a theologically practical way.[29]

For Bloesch, biblical spirituality is oriented towards the prodigious works of God in a particular story. Rather than emphasize the improvement of the soul as in mysticism, Bloesch focuses on "the life-giving flow of the revelation of God in a particular person—Jesus of Nazareth."[30] In this description, one can perceive the attempt to ground spirituality directly in divine written revelation.

Indeed, spirituality for Bloesch is vitally dependent on the story the Bible tells. Of the two, however, only revelation is perfect and divine; spirituality is human and imperfect. Therefore, revelation and spirituality share an unbreakable bond, though in themselves they are different kinds of things. For Bloesch, spirituality is neither the field of revelation nor its focus. Rather, it is a very human response to divine revelation. This means that far from being divine, spirituality partakes of what is relative and

---

27. Ibid., 135.

28. Ibid., 135–36.

29. While I could have used any number of authors who have written on Christian spirituality, I have chosen Bloesch because in large part his view grows out of an in-depth interaction with both contemporary evangelical rationalism and neo-pietist experientialism. Indeed, as can be seen throughout the present book, his writings have informed my own views.

30. Bloesch, *Spirituality Old and New*, 39.

fallible.³¹ "True spirituality" is anchored in a theology that produces living faith in the God and Father of our Lord Jesus Christ. This faith leads us to have a caring concern for the good of our neighbor that exceeds the perfections of our inner life.³²

Bloesch breaks down his position as follows: the Bible has to do with logos, while spirituality is oriented to praxis. Biblical spirituality is therefore a two-sided coin. The biblical side is focused on the truth and confession of faith, while the spiritual side stresses the life and experience of faith. The spiritual person, therefore, is in a constant search for both truth and holy obedience. The task of theology is to maintain the integrity of the faith in the midst of a skeptical world, while that of spirituality is to render our faith concretely in works of love. "Dogma and praxis are inseparable; one leads into the other."³³

According to this model, biblical spirituality overcomes the Neoplatonic reductionism that plagues doctrinalist and experientialist approaches. It accomplishes this by rescuing spirituality from what is essentially a mystical preoccupation with the immaterial self and returning it to practical bodily life. Biblical spirituality avoids notions of spirituality as altered states of consciousness through quietist practices on the one side and enthusiast concerns on the other. It circumvents the idea of spirituality as the infusion of God's presence directly into the soul, but it also makes a proper distinction between logos (theology) and praxis (spirituality) without polarizing them. To be spiritual in the biblical sense is not a question of experiencing ecstasy, possessing supernatural gifts, knowing the biblical doctrines in detail, or speaking powerfully. If these were the conditions, only a few believers would be predisposed towards spirituality. Furthermore, it would be a strictly personal affair, whereas the Holy Spirit teaches that spirituality is made perfect in the collective sphere.

As mentioned above, biblical spirituality has to do primarily with daily, obedient living under the authority of the Spirit of Christ. While Bloesch rightly stresses the foundational importance of written revelation for spirituality, we need to bring balance to this aspect by stressing the

---

31. Ibid., 26.

32. Ibid., 29. Schneiders also places emphasis on the practical aspect of faith in her definition, writing that Christian spirituality is "a self-transcending faith in which union with God in Jesus Christ through the Spirit expresses itself in service of the neighbor and participation in the realization of the reign of God in this world" (Schneiders, "Biblical Spirituality," 134).

33. Bloesch, *Spirituality Old and New*, 28–29.

living lordship of the Spirit. To fail to do so is to risk giving the impression that spirituality consists in sincere and well-meaning attempts to put the teachings of the Bible into practice. Submission to Scripture through the Spirit, but also to the guidance of the Spirit in accordance with Scripture, makes up our daily spirituality.

The Biblical Data

I wanted to spend a little time interacting with Bloesch because it seems to me that his theological reflections cover the fundamental elements of an evangelical spirituality. Having conferred with Bloesch so that we might confront our own presuppositions and ideas with a well-thought-out, representative scheme of biblical spirituality, we are better positioned to look critically at what the Bible actually teaches on the subject.

As I have already stated, the term "spirituality" has its origins in the Bible, even though the noun never appears there. It goes back to the Hebrew word *ruach* found in the Old Testament, where it means "breath," "wind," or "spirit." The identification of *ruach* with "breath" will prove to be particularly important, as it connects the developing biblical image of "spirit" with the notion of "life."

The English word "spiritual" appears for the first time in the New Testament and is the translation of the Greek adjective *pneumatikos*. The various forms of the word occur more than twenty times, almost exclusively in the writings of Paul. In the most general sense, it means that which concerns or belongs to the spirit. Stating the lexical meaning of the term, however, does not in itself avail us all that much for understanding biblical spirituality; there remains the contextual question of what *pneumatikos* refers to in any given appearance in the Bible: the Spirit of God, the spirit of man, or immateriality in general.

Some argue that it is used primarily to distinguish what belongs to the supernatural world from what is of the natural world. Passages often cited in proof of this view are verses 44 and 46 of 1 Cor 15, where Paul makes a clear distinction between the natural body (*soma psukikon*) of the present time and the spiritual body (*soma pneumatikon*) of the resurrection. The point emphasized is that *pneumatikos* has to do mainly with the immaterial in contrast with the material.[34] Having worked extensively on the *pneuma* word group in Paul's letters, however, Gordon Fee objects. In

---

34. Friberg and Friberg, "πνευματικός."

his own study, Fee became "more and more distressed by our translating the adjective *pneumatikos* with a small-case letter, 'spiritual.'"[35] The reason for Fee's uncertainty is his conclusion that the Greek word *pneumatikos* in New Testament Pauline usage "has the Holy Spirit as its primary referent."[36] Fee goes on to point out that Paul never uses the adjective to refer to the human spirit, and neither does he use it in the more general sense as referring to "some unseen reality in contrast to, for example, something material, secular, ritual, or tangible."[37] Summing up his conclusion of the *pneuma* word group, Fee writes:

> In the New Testament, therefore, spirituality is defined altogether in terms of the Spirit of God (or Christ). One is spiritual to the degree that one lives in and walks by the Spirit; in Scripture the word has no other meaning, and no other measurement.[38]

The meaning of *pneumatikos* in Pauline literature, especially in First Corinthians, continues to be a contentious issue in the larger debate.[39] Nevertheless, an analysis of the relevant biblical passages appears to favor Fee's conclusions. At the very least, it can be argued that there are no special cases where the inclusion of the Holy Spirit as the referent of "spiritual" is harmful to either the immediate context of the passages in question or the biblical context as a whole.[40]

---

35. Fee, *Listening to the Spirit*, 5.

36. Ibid. For Fee's fullest statement on this topic, see Fee, *God's Empowering Presence*. See also Fee, *First Epistle to the Corinthians*.

37. Fee, *Listening to the Spirit*, 5.

38. Ibid.

39. Part of the problem is determining how the Corinthians were using *pneumatikos* (and *psychikos*) and from what source(s) they derived this meaning. Consequently, the major portion of the literature dealing with these questions has sought to determine the meaning of Paul's use of the terms by comparing the contemporary extra-biblical parallel sources that had supposedly influenced the Corinthians' usage that Paul was attempting to correct. This venture has not always been successful, however. For a critique of this view, see, e.g., Horsley, "Pneumatikos vs Psychikos." Others argue that the immediate contexts of First Corinthians in which the terms are used are sufficient to clarify Paul's usage without having to propose theories about their origins or prior use. See, for example, Johnson, "Turning the World Upside Down," 292. Anthony Thiselton seems to take a middle ground by distinguishing between how the Corinthians may have been using *pneumatikos* and Paul's redefinition of it (Thiselton, *First Epistle to the Corinthians*, 225).

40. One clear exception would be Eph 6:12: "the spiritual forces of evil in the heavenly places." In this passage, the referent of *pneumatikos* is clearly not the Spirit of God but rather the immaterial satanic forces of the heavenly places. For in-depth though differing

DOCTRINE AND EXPERIENCE

Thus, when Paul writes of "spiritual gifts" in 1 Cor 12:1 and 14:1, he understands them as spiritual because they are ministered by and pertaining to the operation of the Holy Spirit (1 Cor 12:11). Similarly, the claim that the law is spiritual in Rom 7:14 clearly does not mean that the law is immaterial or has to do with the human spirit, but rather that it is an expression of God's righteousness given through the ministry of the Holy Spirit (cf. Rom 8:3–4). As Anthony Thiselton points out, in 1 Cor 10:1–4 Paul wants to ensure his readers understand that even the ancient Jews had been subject to Christ *facto ex ante* (before the event). Paul reminds them that their ancestors in the faith ate the same "spiritual food" (the manna from heaven) and drank the same "spiritual drink" (the rock struck by Moses) not in order to say that these were immaterial things but rather to show that they had been provided by the Holy Spirit.[41]

It is generally agreed that the most important text for understanding the meaning of *pneumatikos* is in the second chapter of First Corinthians:

> And we impart this in words not taught by human wisdom but taught by the Spirit, interpreting spiritual [*pneumatikois*] truths to those who are spiritual [*pneumataka*]. The natural [*psychikos*] person does not accept the things of the Spirit of God [*pneumatos tou theou*], for they are folly to him, and he is not able to understand them because they are spiritually [*pneumatikos*] discerned. The spiritual [*pneumatikos*] person judges all things, but is himself to be judged by no one. "For who has understood the mind of the Lord so as to instruct him?" But we have the mind of Christ. But I, brothers, could not address you as spiritual [*pneumatikois*] people, but as people of the flesh [*sarkinois*], as infants in Christ. I fed you with milk, not solid food, for you were not ready for it. And even now you are not yet ready, for you are still of the flesh [*sarkikos*]. For while there is jealousy and strife among you, are you not of the flesh [*sarkikos*] and behaving only in a human way? (1 Cor 2:13—3:3)

It is likely that in this passage Paul was writing with irony, using language the Corinthians themselves would have used to argue about who was the most spiritual among them.[42] Therefore, Paul used such terms as "spiri-

---

views on the identities of these spiritual forces, see Berkhof, *Christ and the Powers*; Yoder, *Politics of Jesus*.

41. Thiselton, *First Epistle to the Corinthians*, 726.

42. Paul uses this method elsewhere in the letter, using the precise vocabulary of the Corinthians as a rhetorical device. See 1 Cor 6:12–10: 23; 7:1, 8:1, 4.

tual," "natural," and "carnal" strategically in order to criticize the behavior of these immature believers. For this reason, we must be careful not to take Paul's argument as if it were a dispassionate treatise on spirituality and carnality. Paul was being polemical and practical; he was not so directly concerned with a detailed theological analysis of the believer's position in Christ as he was with rebuking the Corinthians in the hope that they would reflect on their distinctly un-Spirit-like behavior in order to change it.

However, far from being a hindrance, Paul's method and objectives are crucial in establishing a biblical theology of spirituality, for they help us to understand that, strictly speaking, spirituality has more to do with the believer's daily walk in obedience to the Holy Spirit than either the believer's positional standing in Christ or some ethereal elevation of his or her inner state of consciousness. Concerning the latter, Bernard McGinn comes to the same conclusion when he reminds us that the opposition between carnal (*sarkinois*) and spiritual persons (*pneumatikos*) in 1 Cor 3:1 did not originally have to do with a Platonic dualism that contrasts the body and soul "but rather addressed the concrete human choices between life lived according to egoistic satisfaction and that conducted according to God's purpose."[43] James Wiseman agrees, writing that the "flesh" was not understood as the physical human body that stood in opposition to the spirit but rather as the base nature of individualistic creatures. To "live according to the flesh," therefore, meant to live by the purely selfish inclinations that are inevitable in those who are immature in the faith. Spiritual persons, on the other hand, are simply those who are open to the Spirit of God.[44]

These observations are important because they help us avoid the spiritualistic tendencies of much contemporary experientialism. Among charismatics and non-charismatics alike, there are two important misconceptions concerning the question at hand. First, carnality and spirituality are sometimes understood as a question of *possession*—that is, the carnal believer possesses less of the Spirit and more of the flesh, while the spiritual person boasts of having a greater portion of the Holy Spirit. The major theological error in this way of thinking is that, as we have already seen, the Bible presents carnality as our own egotistical self lived out through the body in practice, and in spirituality as practical submission of the entire person to Christ through the Spirit. Thus, we are not dealing with a question of ownership or even stewardship but rather of obedience and disobedience,

---

43. McGinn, "Letter and the Spirit," 14.
44. Wiseman, *Spirituality and Mysticism*, 2.

for people are carnal not because they have flesh but because they have not died to it and so act according to the un-crucified self. On the other hand, true believers all possess the Holy Spirit in the same measure, but this fact alone does not make them equally spiritual according to Paul's argument in Corinthians. Rather, what makes believers spiritual is the practical, daily obedience to the Spirit of the crucified self.

A second error in contemporary experientialist interpretations of spirituality is a propensity to overlook the role of the flesh altogether and attribute carnal behavior to the operations of evil spirits at work directly in and/or upon believers. According to this model, demons are the immediate cause of our sins; we are but victims. In order to reverse this situation, we must become powerful in the Spirit. To achieve this, the believer needs to enter into the "spiritual domain" (rather than stand against it), in order to fight the forces of darkness by yielding the weapons of faith, prayer, fasting, watching, and authoritative intimidation of the evil spirits through vocal assaults in Jesus' name. Contrary to biblical teaching, this position does away with the flesh and conceives of the devil as the Spirit's main foil. According to this anthropology, carnal behavior is not really carnal at all but demonic.[45] This is very different from the biblical teaching that understands our own un-crucified, concupiscent self as the immediate cause of unspiritual behavior and sees the devil as an opportunistic *provocateur* of the flesh.[46]

To be fleshly, according to the Bible, is simply to act as the world does in accordance with its *un-Spirited* nature—that is, in opposition to the life that "is correctly integrated into and dominated by God's spiritual Kingdom."[47] To recognize that spirituality is the daily-dying self's trusting,

---

45. A passage continuously abused to wrongly prove this point is 1 Pet 5:8, which affirms that the devil prowls around like a roaring lion looking for someone to devour. The context of this statement, however, is Christian persecution and not spiritual versus carnal behavior per se.

46. In Eph 4:26–27, Paul exhorts the believers to give no opportunity to the devil by allowing their flesh to win the day, suggesting that the devil's influence in determining the believer's behavior is directly related to the degree to which the self has not been crucified. James' appeal in 4:7 for his readers to resist the devil so that he might flee from them is also couched in the context of "crucifying the flesh" language. Resistance here is clearly not understood as shouting at the devil in Jesus' name but rather as humbling (Jas 4:6, 8a) and purifying oneself from adulterous actions (Jas 4:8b) in profound repentance (Jas 4:9).

47. Willard, *Spirit of the Disciplines*, 67.

Spirituality Caught in the Crossfire of Doctrine and Experience

practical obedience to the Holy Spirit is nothing less than liberation into the fullness of God's life.

That such a view of spirituality is indeed the biblical view is confirmed by how Paul equates "spirituality" with Christian "maturity" rather than with an elevated state of the soul by either infusion of more Spirit or the exorcism of spirits.[48] Thus, Paul does not describe the Corinthians as people who have less Holy Spirit, more demons, or an inferior quality of soul than other Christians but rather "as people *of* the flesh"—immature, selfish, "infant" Christians (1 Cor 3:1). To affirm that Paul is comparing those who have more Holy Spirit to those who have more flesh is wrong. The contrast is instead between those who have the Spirit and live for others and those who live for themselves despite having the same Spirit.[49] Wiseman summa-

---

48. Richard Horsley writes, "Paul uses the term 'spiritual people' (*pneumatikoi*) as an apparent synonym for 'mature.' This indicates that the contrast in 2:14-15 between 'those who are spiritual' and 'those who are unspiritual' (*psychikoi*) is parallel and synonymous to the distinction between 'mature' (2:6) and 'infants' (3:1)" (Horsley, *1 Corinthians*, 57).

49. Referring to 1 Cor 2:6–3:4, Andrew Naselli contests the claim that there exist distinct categories of "spiritual Christians" and "carnal Christians." Rather, he asserts that all Christians are spiritual, insofar as in Christ they all have the Spirit (Naselli, "Keswick Theology," 38–39). According to the standard Naselli sets up, he is of course correct. The question, however, is if his demarcation of category lines up with Paul's intent in the Corinthian passage. Naselli's main contention is that Paul is not addressing the Corinthian believers "as who they actually are." But this claim seems to fly in the face of Paul's argument that the Corinthians should be more mature than they presently are. Furthermore, it presupposes a kind of Neoplatonic dualism that assumes that how one actually behaves has nothing to do with who one is. But can it be biblically supported, for example, that a Christian is not a thief, even though she is stealing? Likewise, is it the case that a believer is not envious, even though his every thought is filled with envy? If there are categories of "Christian thief" and "envious Christian," is there not also an ontological category of "carnal believer" based on one's way of being or living? We have to admit that while still in the present "body of death" there will be differences between what we are by virtue of our position in Christ and what we do in practice, but does this warrant Naselli's stark dualism between being and doing? The sinner *is* redeemed, but the redeemed *are* at the same time sinners (Luther). To stress positional sanctification to the point that one can say, "I am spiritual, though my deeds are carnal," is the kind of wrongful boasting Paul condemns throughout the letter (see chapter 3 above). Naselli denounces (in an overstatement, I believe) that Keswick teaches that believers categorized as "carnal" are signaled out as lesser Christians because they are less spiritual. However, to affirm a category of "carnal Christians" does not presuppose that any particular Christian who is carnal is *intrinsically* inferior to a spiritual Christian any more than a child who belongs to the category of "immature children" is intrinsically inferior to a mature child. Paul is not arguing substance ontology here. Thus, Naselli's dualistic tendencies result in a "soft" category mistake. Paul sets up the categories of "spiritual" and "carnal" not to speak of position or intrinsic worth but of actual behavior. In addition, he establishes behavioral

rizes this position by writing that the mature disciple lives "according to the promptings of God's Spirit, whose fruit he describes in another of his letters as 'love, joy, peace, patience, kindness, generosity, faithfulness, gentleness, and self-control' (Gal 5:22)."[50] Wiseman concludes his evaluation with the following observations:

> For a follower of Christ to live in such a way is a preeminent mark of what Paul means by "a spiritual person." This brings us back to that root meaning of *spiritualis* as "pertaining to breathing" and hence to life, which is why Paul can very readily refer to God's Spirit as "the Spirit of life," as when he writes to the Romans that "the law of the Spirit of life in Christ Jesus has set you free from the law of sin and of death" (Rom 8:2).[51]

In Paul's letter to the Romans, in fact, Paul does not present the conflict between spirituality and carnality in terms of a contest between two separate entities that live inside each person but rather as a mind that is either surrendered to the guidance of the Spirit or to the desires of the flesh: "For those who live according to the flesh set their minds on the things of the flesh, but those who live according to the Spirit set their minds on the things of the Spirit" (Rom 8:5). This idea is just as clear in Galatians, where the battle line is drawn between walking by the Spirit and walking by the flesh. Those who walk by the Spirit do not fulfill their selfish desires, simply because by the power of the Holy Spirit, they put Christ's will into practice in place of their own natural will. In other words, carnal believers still live like worldly people—that is to say, according to their own interests. Spiritual people, on the other hand, have put their natural selves to death in submission to the will of the Spirit (Gal 5:16–17; cf. Rom 8:13).

The biblical picture of spirituality, therefore, shows a gradual formation of the person, but not in the sense of passing from one *level* of spirituality to the next. It is a process that works from the inside out, but it does not distinguish between higher and lower *states* of our inner being, strictly speaking, for years of obedience to God can be unraveled in a moment of unrepentant disobedience. There is no fixed inner state of irreversible

---

categories such that whoever is behaving according to the Spirit is in the spiritual category and whoever is living selfishly is in the carnal category. Furthermore, to impose a positional meaning on the passage cuts across the inspired writer's intent in the context of the entire epistle—namely, pointing out his readers' carnality so that they might repent and walk spiritually.

50. Wiseman, *Spirituality and Mysticism*, 2.
51. Ibid.

spirituality to achieve. Rather, the goal of biblical spirituality is the believer's steady availability to the lordship of the Spirit, or, as the Scriptures put it, a pure heart that hears and obeys and then acts through the body in accordance to the word of Christ. Thus, the Scripture does not isolate the interior life from the rest of the person as if the soul alone could be nourished without reference to the body.[52] Dallas Willard summarizes this point eloquently:

> Spirituality in human beings is not an extra or "superior" mode of existence. It's not a hidden stream of separate reality, a separate life running parallel to our bodily existence. It does not consist of special "inward" acts even though it has an inner aspect. It is, rather, a relationship of our embodied selves to God that has the natural and irrepressible effect of making us alive to the Kingdom of God—here and now in the material world.[53]

The biblical witness understands spirituality as a walk of faith rather than as a constant search for various experiences to confirm the truth of that faith.[54] Spirituality, as presented in written revelation, demands obedience to God, even though we are not capable of always understanding fully what is required. On the other hand, the kind of spirituality that focuses on the experiences of God is not based on faith but on sight. The Christian philosopher Jacques Ellul has even identified a root of concupiscence in experiential spirituality, insofar as it is based on a desire to be in possession of God through what can be experienced of him. And, as Ellul points out, what we experience, we possess.[55]

On the contrary, a spirituality based on biblical faith does not attempt to possess but to obey God. It is not self-centered but Christ-centered. Much that passes for Christian spirituality today, especially among experientialists, is a mixture of biblical spirituality and the "new spirituality," as Bloesch calls it. Some elements of this new spirituality are that it glorifies

---

52. One could well ask what such disengagement might even look like in practice, given that without a physical brain connected to a central nervous system, one would be hard-pressed to even conceive of a human consciousness to alter. This is not to say that in biblical spirituality no actual changes occur in the inner person as we grow spiritually, it simply implies that these transformations cannot be independent of the participation of the normal functions of the human body.

53. Willard, *Spirit of the Disciplines*, 31.

54. Bloesch, *Spirituality Old and New*, 27.

55. Jacques Ellul, *The Humiliation of the Word* (Grand Rapids: Eerdmans, 1985), 192, cited in Bloesch, *Spirituality Old and New*, 27.

rather than sacrifices self, it encourages us to explore the power of the mind as opposed to bringing the mind into conformity with Christ, and it is individualistic and looks for hidden knowledge.[56] The compromises of the new spirituality can be seen in churches where praise is practiced to the detriment of petition and supplication; where the pursuit of health, wealth, and prosperity becomes fundamental Christian doctrine; wherever personal and spiritual renewal is seen in terms of higher states of consciousness or spirituality; and in communities affected by the emerging church that deviate toward mysticism and undetermined relativism.

A biblical spirituality, on the other hand, is cross-shaped. It is through the cross that the Spirit becomes Guide, Lord, and Life to the believer. Accordingly, the main objective of biblical spirituality is not to have many experiences of the Spirit but to spend oneself in obeying him so that he might not be grieved. This inevitably entails renouncing self for the good of others. Biblically spiritual people, therefore, are geared towards transforming the world and not themselves. They will be transformed, but only by dying to themselves rather than by being taken up in rapturous experiences. Change occurs when we look not to ourselves but to Jesus (2 Cor 3:18). We give up self in order to do the will of God (Rom 12:1–2). True spirituality does not take us out of the world in ecstasy but rather challenges us to bring the world into submission to the Lord Jesus Christ.[57]

We might add that this can only be accomplished through the power of the Spirit as Lord operating in a life surrendered to God's word.

---

56. Bloesch, *Spirituality Old and New*, 31–32.
57. Ibid., 41.

Bibliography

Adam, A. K. M. *Faithful Interpretation: Reading the Bible in a Postmodern World.* Minneapolis: Fortress, 2006.

Alexander, Archibald. "An Inaugural Discourse." In *The Sermon Delivered at the Inauguration of the Rev. Archibald Alexander, P. P., as Professor of Didactic and Polemic Theology: In the Theological Seminary of the Presbyterian Church in the United States of America*, 55–104. New York: Whiting & Watson, 1812.

Augustine. *Treatise on the Predestination of the Saints.* In vol. 5 of *The Nicene and Post-Nicene Fathers*, Series 1. Edited by Philip Schaff. 14 vols. Peabody, MA: Hendrickson, 1994.

Barth, Karl. *Protestant Theology in the Nineteenth Century: Its Background and History.* Valley Forge, PA: Judson, 1959.

Battle, John A. "Charles Hodge, Inspiration, Textual Criticism, and the Princeton Doctrine of Scripture." *Western Reformed Seminary Journal* 4, no. 2 (1997) 28–41.

Bauckham, Richard J. "Theology of the Cross." Edited by Sinclair B. Ferguson, David F. Wright, and J. I. Packer. *New Dictionary of Theology*. Downers Grove, IL: InterVarsity, 1988.

Becker, Matthew L. *Fundamental Theology: A Protestant Perspective.* London: Bloomsbury, 2014.

Bennett, Charles N. "Karl Barth's Critique of Pietism: A Challenge to Contemporary Christians." *Journal of Theta Alpha Kappa* 9, no. 2 (1985) 30–36.

Berkhof, Hendrikus. *Christ and the Powers.* Scottdale, PA: Herald, 1962.

Bloesch, Donald G. *The Christian Life and Salvation.* Colorado Springs, CO: Helmers & Howard, 1991.

———. *The Church: Sacraments, Worship, Ministry, Mission.* Christian Foundations. Downers Grove, IL: InterVarsity, 2002.

———. *The Crisis of Piety: Essays Towards a Theology of the Christian Life.* 2nd ed. Colorado Springs, CO: Helmers & Howard, 1988.

———. "Donald Bloesch Responds." In *Evangelical Theology in Transition: Theologians in Dialogue with Donald Bloesch*, edited by Elmer M. Colyer, 183–208. Downers Grove, IL: InterVarsity, 1999.

———. *The Future of Evangelical Christianity: A Call for Unity Amid Diversity.* 1st ed. Garden City, NY: Doubleday, 1983.

———. *God, Authority, and Salvation*. Vol. 1 of *Essentials of Evangelical Theology*. 2 vols. San Francisco: Harper & Row, 1978.

———. *The Ground of Certainty: Toward an Evangelical Theology of Revelation*. Grand Rapids: Eerdmans, 1971.

———. *The Holy Spirit: Works and Gifts*. Christian Foundations. Downers Grove, IL: InterVarsity, 2000.

———. *Life, Ministry, and Hope*. Vol. 2 of *Essentials of Evangelical Theology*. 2 vols. San Francisco: Harper & Row, 1979.

———. *Spirituality Old and New: Recovering Authentic Spiritual Life*. Downers Grove, IL: InterVarsity Academic, 2007.

———. *A Theology of Word and Spirit: Authority and Method in Theology*. Christian Foundations. Downers Grove, IL: InterVarsity, 2005.

Bowers, Amanda. "False Teachings About Hearing Audible Words from God Taking Even Deeper Root in Today's Church." *Sola Sisters*. February 15, 2012. http://www.solasisters.com/2012/02/cant-hear-god-speak-repent-says-henry.html.

Braaten, Carl E. *Because of Christ: Memoirs of a Lutheran Theologian*. Grand Rapids: Eerdmans, 2010.

Bregman, Lucy. "Defining Spirituality: Multiple Uses and Murky Meanings of an Incredibly Popular Term." *Journal of Pastoral Care and Counseling* 58, no. 3 (2004) 157–67.

Breward, I. "Puritan Theology." In *New Dictionary of Theology*, edited by Sinclair B. Ferguson, David F. Wright, and J. I. Packer. Downers Grove, IL: InterVarsity, 1988.

Brown, Dale W. *Understanding Pietism*. Grand Rapids: Eerdmans, 1978.

Brown, Raymond E. *An Introduction to the New Testament*. New York: Doubleday, 1997.

Bruner, Frederick Dale. *A Theology of the Holy Spirit: The Pentecostal Experience and the New Testament Witness*. Grand Rapids: Eerdmans, 1970.

Cairns, Earle E. *Christianity through the Centuries: A History of the Christian Church*. 3rd ed. Grand Rapids: Zondervan, 1996.

Carson, D. A. *A Call to Spiritual Reformation: Priorities from Paul and His Prayers*. Reprint ed. Grand Rapids: Baker Academic, 1992.

———. "The Spirituality of the Gospel of John: Part 1." Lecture, June 14, 2014. http://resources.thegospelcoalition.org/library/the-spirituality-of-the-gospel-of-john-part-1.

———. "When Is Spirituality Spiritual? Reflections on Some Problems of Definition." *Journal of the Evangelical Theological Society* 37, no. 3 (1994) 381–94.

Carson, D. A., et al., eds. *New Bible Commentary: 21st Century Edition*. Leicester, UK: InterVarsity, 1994.

Chan, Simon, and W. R. Ward. "Pietism." In *Global Dictionary of Theology: A Resource for the Worldwide Church*, edited by William A. Dyrness, Veli-Matti Kärkkäinen, Juan F. Martinez, and Simon Chan. Downers Grove, IL: InterVarsity Academic, 2008.

Clifton, Shane. *Pentecostal Churches in Transition: Analysing the Developing Ecclesiology of the Assemblies of God in Australia*. Leiden: Brill, 2009.

Cole, Graham. "Sola Scriptura: Some Historical and Contemporary Perspectives." *Churchman* 104, no. 1 (1990) 20–34.

Collins, Kenneth J. "What Is Spirituality? Historical and Methodological Considerations." *Wesleyan Theological Journal* 31, no. 1 (1996) 76–94.

Colyer, Elmer M., ed. *Evangelical Theology in Transition: Theologians in Dialogue with Donald Bloesch*. Downers Grove, IL: InterVarsity, 1999.

Bibliography

Conn, Harvie M. *Contemporary World Theology: A Layman's Guidebook.* Nutley, NJ: Presbyterian & Reformed, 1973.

Corduan, Winfried. *Mysticism: An Evangelical Option?* Eugene, OR: Wipf & Stock, 1991.

Craigie, Peter. *Psalms 1–50.* Nashville: Nelson, 1983.

Davids, Peter H. "Signs and Wonders." In *Dictionary of the Later New Testament and Its Developments*, edited by Ralph P. Martin and Peter H. Davids. Downers Grove, IL: InterVarsity, 1997.

Dayton, Donald W. "Theological Roots of Pentecostalism." *Pneuma* 2, no. 1 (1980) 3–21.

Dyrness, William A., Veli-Matti Kärkkäinen, Juan F. Martinez, and Simon Chan, eds. *Global Dictionary of Theology: A Resource for the Worldwide Church.* Downers Grove, IL: InterVarsity Academic, 2008.

Dulles, Avery. *Models of Revelation.* Garden City, NY: Doubleday, 1983.

Dunn, James D. G. "Prayer." In *Dictionary of Jesus and the Gospels*, edited by Joel B. Green, Scot McKnight, and I. Howard Marshall. Downers Grove, IL: InterVarsity, 1992.

Encyclopædia Britannica Online, s. v. "Romanticism." Accessed December 19, 2015. http://www.britannica.com/art/Romanticism.

Erickson, Millard J. "Donald Bloesch's Doctrine of Scripture." In *Evangelical Theology in Transition: Theologians in Dialogue with Donald Bloesch*, edited by Elmer M. Colyer, 77–97. Downers Grove, IL: InterVarsity, 1999.

———. *The Evangelical Left: Encountering Postconservative Evangelical Theology.* Grand Rapids: Baker, 1997.

———. *Postmodernizing the Faith: Evangelical Responses to the Challenge of Postmodernism.* Grand Rapids: Baker, 1998.

Eskridge, Larry. "Pentecostalism and the Charismatic Movement." *Institute for the Sutdy of American Evangelicals.* Last modified 2012. http://www.wheaton.edu/ISAE/Defining-Evangelicalism/Pentecostalism.

Fanning, B. M. "Word." In *New Dictionary of Biblical Theology*, edited by T. Desmond Alexander and Brian S. Rosner. Leicester, UK: InterVarsity, 2000.

Fee, Gordon D. *The First Epistle to the Corinthians.* Grand Rapids: Eerdmans, 1987.

———. "Gifts of the Spirit." In *Dictionary of Paul and His Letters*, edited by Gerald F. Hawthorne, Ralph P. Martin, and Daniel G. Reid. Downers Grove, IL: InterVarsity, 1993.

———. *God's Empowering Presence: The Holy Spirit in the Letters of Paul.* Peabody, MA: Hendrickson, 1994.

———. *Listening to the Spirit in the Text.* Grand Rapids: Eerdmans, 2000.

Fitzmeyer, Joseph A. *First Corinthians.* New Haven: Yale University Press, 2007.

Foss, Michael W. "Rethinking the Mystical: Thoughts from the Spiritual Closet—An Evangelical Perspective." *Word and World* 7, no. 2 (1987) 148–52.

Fowl, Stephen E. "Imitation of Paul/of Christ." In *Dictionary of Paul and His Letters*, edited by Gerald F. Hawthorne, Ralph P. Martin, and Daniel G. Reid. Downers Grove, IL: InterVarsity, 1993.

Franco, Francesco. "Schleiermacher Friedrich." In *Lexicon: Dizionario Dei Teologi*, edited by Luciano Pacomio and Giuseppe Occhipinti, 1121–24. Casale Monferrato, Italy: Piemme, 1998.

Friberg, Timothy, and Barbara Friberg. *Analytical Greek New Testament* [*GNM*]. 2nd ed. n.p.: BibleWorks 6, 1994.

———. "πνευματικός." *Analytical Greek New Testament* [*GNM*]. n.p.: BibleWorks 6, 1994.

Bibliography

George, Timothy. "Reading the Bible with the Reformers." *First Things*, no. 211 (2011) 27–33.

Gilley, Gary. "Contemplative Prayer." *Think on These Things* 18, no. 2 (2012). http://www.svchapel.org/resources/articles/133-spiritual-formation-movement/761-contemplative-prayer.

Goldingay, John. *Psalms 1–41*. Vol. 1 of *Psalms*. Grand Rapids: Baker, 2006.

González, Justo L. *Essential Theological Terms*. 1st ed. Louisville: Westminster John Knox, 2005.

Greidanus, Sydney. "The Nature of Paul's Letters." In *Dictionary of Paul and His Letters*, edited by Gerald F. Hawthorne, Ralph P. Martin, and Daniel G. Reid. Downers Grove, IL: InterVarsity, 1993.

Grenz, Stanley J. *Renewing the Center: Evangelical Theology in a Post-Theological Era*. Grand Rapids: Baker, 2000.

Grenz, Stanley J., and John R. Franke. *Beyond Foundationalism: Shaping Theology in a Postmodern Context*. Louisville: Westminster John Knox, 2001.

Groothuis, Douglas. *Truth Decay: Defending Christianity Against the Challenges of Postmodernism*. Downers Grove, IL: InterVarsity, 2000.

Hansen, Collin, and John D. Woodbridge. *A God-Sized Vision: Revival Stories That Stretch and Stir*. Grand Rapids: Zondervan, 2010.

Harris, Harriet A. *Fundamentalism and Evangelicals*. Oxford: Oxford University Press, 1998.

Hauerwas, Stanley. *Unleashing the Scripture: Freeing the Bible from Captivity to America*. Nashville: Abingdon, 1993.

Helmer, Christine. *Theology and the End of Doctrine*. Louisville: Westminster John Knox, 2014.

Hesselink, John. "Some Distinctive Contributions of the Dutch-American Reformed Tradition." In *Toward the Future of Reformed Theology: Tasks, Topics, Traditions*, edited by David Willis-Watkins, Michael Welker, and Matthias Gockel, 421–43. Grand Rapids: Eerdmans, 1999.

Hill, Daniel. "Proposition." In *Dictionary for Theological Interpretation of the Bible*, edited by Kevin J. Vanhoozer. Grand Rapids: SPCK, 2005.

Hocken, Peter. "The Pentecostal-Charismatic Movement as Revival and Renewal." *Pneuma* 3, no. 1 (1981) 31–47.

Hodge, Charles. *Systematic Theology*. Vol. 1. Grand Rapids: Eerdmans, 1940.

Hoffman, Mark Vitalis. "The Bible as Word of God." *Word and World* 32, no. 4 (2012) 348–55.

Holmes, Stephen R. *Listening to the Past: The Place of Tradition in Theology*. Carlisle, UK: Paternoster, 2002.

Holmes, Urban T., III. *A History of Christian Spirituality: An Analytical Introduction*. Library of Episcopalian Classics. Harrisburg, PA: Morehouse, 2002.

Horsley, Richard A. *1 Corinthians*. Abingdon New Testament Commentaries. Nashville: Abingdon, 1998.

———. "Pneumatikos vs. Psychikos: Distinctions of Spiritual Status Among the Corinthians." *Harvard Theological Review* 69, no. 3–4 (1976) 269–88.

Introvigne, Massimo, and PierLuigi Zoccatelli. "Le origini pentecostali." *Le religioni in Italia*, December 17, 2015. http://www.cesnur.org/religioni_italia/p/pentecostali_01.htm.

Bibliography

———."Il terzo protestantesimo: le Chiese libere e il movimento holiness." *Le religioni in Italia*. Last modified December 17, 2015. http://www.cesnur.org/religioni_italia/p/protestantesimo3_06.htm.

———. "La terza ondata: (a) Vineyard e i risvegli di Toronto e Pensacola." *Le religioni in Italia*. Last modified December 17, 2015. http://www.cesnur.com/la-terza-ondata-a-vineyard-e-i-risvegli-di-toronto-e-pensacola/.

———. "La terza ondata: (b) il Movimento della Fede." *Le religioni in Italia*. Last modified December 17, 2015. http://www.cesnur.com/?s=la+terza+ondata.

Johnson, Andrew. "Turning the World Upside Down in 1 Corinthians 15: Apocalyptic Epistemology, the Resurrected Body and the New Creation." *Evangelical Quarterly* 75, no. 4 (2003) 291.

Johnson, Arthur L. *Faith Misguided: Exposing the Dangers of Mysticism*. Chicago: Moody, 1988.

———. "Mysticism and Evangelical Thought." *Bulletin of the Evangelical Philosophical Society* 8 (1985) 18–27.

Johnson, Keith E. "Trinitarian Agency and the Eternal Subordination of the Son: An Augustinian Perspective." *Themelios* 36, no. 1 (2011) 7–25.

Keener, Craig S. "Power of Pentecost: Luke's Missiology in Acts 1–2." *Asian Journal of Pentecostal Studies* 12, no. 1 (2009) 47–73.

Kempis, Thomas à. *The Imitation of Christ*. Translated by Aloysius Croft and Harold Bolton. Mineola, NY: Dover, 2003.

Kendell, R. T. "Dear Dr. MacArthur." *R. T. Kendell Ministries*. November 16, 2013. https://rtkendallministries.com/dear-dr-macarthur.

Kim, Dongsoo. "Johannine Root of Pentecostalism: Johannine Self-Understanding as an Archetype of Pentecostal Self-Understanding." *Asian Journal of Pentecostal Studies* 9, no. 1 (2006) 5–16.

Klooster, Fred H. "How Reformed Theologians 'Do Theology' in Today's World." In *Doing Theology in Today's World: Essays in Honor of Kenneth S. Kantzer*, edited by John D. Woodbridge and Thomas Edward McComiskey, 227–50. Grand Rapids: Zondervan, 1994.

Land, Steven. *Pentecostal Spirituality: A Passion for the Kingdom*. Cleveland, TN: CPT, 2010.

Lindbeck, George A. *The Nature of Doctrine: Religion and Theology in a Postliberal Age*. Philadelphia: Westminster, 1984.

Lindsell, Harold. *The Battle for the Bible*. Grand Rapids: Zondervan, 1976.

Lloyd-Jones, D. Martyn. *Joy Unspeakable: The Baptism and Gifts of the Holy Spirit*. Eastbourne, UK: Kingsway, 1995.

———. *Revival*. Westchester, IL: Crossway, 1987.

MacArthur, John. "False Prophets and Lying Wonders." *Grace to You* (blog). January 11, 2010. http://www.gty.org/blog/B100111/false-prophets-and-lying-wonders.

Martin, Ralph P. *The Worship of God: Some Theological, Pastoral, and Practical Reflections*. Grand Rapids: Eerdmans, 1982.

Maspero, Giulio, and Robert J. Wozniak, eds. *Rethinking Trinitarian Theology: Disputed Questions and Contemporary Issues in Trinitarian Theology*. London: T&T Clark International, 2012.

McAlpine, Rob. *Post-Charismatic?: Where Are We Now? Where Have We Come From? Where Are We Going?* Eastbourne, UK: David C. Cook, 2008.

Bibliography

McCall, Thomas, and Michael C. Rea, eds. *Philosophical and Theological Essays on the Trinity*. 1st ed. Oxford, UK: Oxford University Press, 2010.

McConnel, Tim. "The Old Princeton Apologetics: Common Sense or Reformed?" *Journal of Evangelical Theological Society* 46, no. 4 (2003) 647–72.

McCormack, Bruce L. "The Being of Holy Scripture Is in Becoming: Karl Barth in Conversation with American Evangelical Criticism." In *Evangelicals and Scripture: Tradition, Authority, and Hermeneutics*, edited by Vincent Bacote, Dennis L. Okholm, and Laura C. Miguélez, 55–75. InterVarsity, 2004.

———. "The Processions Contain the Missions: Reconstructing the Doctrine of an Immanent Trinity." In *The God Who Graciously Elects: Seven Lectures on the Doctrine of God*. Lecture presented at Trinity Evangelical Divinity School, Deerfield, IL, October 3, 2011. http://henrycenter.tiu.edu/resource/processions-contain-missions-doctrine-of-immanent-trinity/.

McGinn, Bernard. "The Letter and the Spirit: Spirituality as an Academic Discipline." *The Cresset*, June 1993, 13–22.

McGrath, Alister E. *Historical Theology: An Introduction to the History of Christian Thought*. Oxford: Blackwell, 1998.

———. "Theology and Experience: Reflections on Cognitive and Experiential Approaches to Theology." *European Journal of Theology* 2, no. 1 (1993) 65–74.

Menzies, Glen W. "A Full Apostolic Gospel Standard of Experience and Doctrine." *Asian Journal of Pentecostal Studies* 15, no. 1 (2012) 19–32.

Menzies, William W. "Non-Wesleyan Pentecostalism: A Tradition the Influence of Fundamentalism." *Asian Journal of Pentecostal Studies* 14, no. 2 (July 2011) 199–211.

———. "The Reformed Roots of Pentecostalism." *Asian Journal of Pentecostal Studies* 9, no. 2 (2006) 260–82.

Morris, Leon. *The Gospel According to John*. Grand Rapids: Eerdmans, 1995.

Murray, Andrew. *The Full Blessing of Pentecost*. 1st ed. Heritage, 2011.

Naselli, Andrew David. "Keswick Theology: A Survey and Analysis of the Doctrine of Sanctification in the Early Keswick Movement." *Detroit Baptist Seminary Journal* 13 (2008) 17–67.

Neff, David. "The Top Books That Have Shaped Evangelicals." *Christianity Today* 50, no. 10 (2006) 51–55.

Nichols, David R. "The Search for a Pentecostal Structure in Systematic Theology." *Pneuma* 6, no. 2 (1984) 57–76.

Noll, Mark A. *The Princeton Theology, 1812–1921: Scripture, Science, and Theological Method from Archibald Alexander to Benjamin Breckinridge Warfield*. Grand Rapids: Baker Academic, 2001.

Ogden, Schubert M. *On Theology*. San Francisco: Harper & Row, 1986.

Olson, Roger E. "A Forum: The Future of Evangelical Theology." *Christianity Today*, February 9, 1998.

———. "Locating Bloesch in the Evangelical Landscape." In *Evangelical Theology in Transition: Theologians in Dialogue with Donald Bloesch*, edited by Elmer M. Colyer. Downers Grove, IL: InterVarsity, 1999.

———. "The Pentecostal Pedigree: How Evangelical. . ." *Christianity Today* 32, no. 11 (1988) 67.

———. "Pietism and Postmodernism: Points of Congeniality." *Christian Scholar's Review* 41, no. 4 (2012) 367–80.

Bibliography

———. *The Story of Christian Theology: Twenty Centuries of Tradition and Reform*. 1st ed. Downers Grove, IL: InterVarsity, 1999.

Osborne, Grant R. *Matthew*. Edited by Clinton E. Arnold. Zondervan Exegetical Commentary Series on the New Testament 1. Grand Rapids: Zondervan, 2010.

Packer, J. I. *Knowing God*. Downers Grove, IL: InterVarsity, 1973.

Pawson, David. *Fourth Wave: Charismatics and Evangelicals, Are We Ready to Come Together?* London: Hodder & Stoughton, 1993.

———. *Word and Spirit Together: Uniting Evangelicals and Charismatics*. 2nd ed. London: Hodder & Stoughton, 1998.

Pelikan, Jaroslav. *The Emergence of the Catholic Tradition (100–600)*. Vol. 1 of *The Christian Tradition: A History of the Development of Doctrine*. Chicago: University of Chicago Press, 1971.

Perkins, Pheme. *First Corinthians*. Grand Rapids: Baker Academic, 2012.

Piper, John. *A Hunger for God: Desiring God through Fasting and Prayer*. Wheaton, IL: Crossway, 1997.

Raschke, Carl A. *The Next Reformation: Why Evangelicals Must Embrace Postmodernity*. Grand Rapids: Baker Academic, 2004.

Saint John of the Cross. *Dark Night of the Soul*. Edited by T. N. R. Rogers and translated by E. Allison Peers. Dover Thrift Editions. Mineola, NY: Dover, 2003.

Schneiders, Sandra M. "Biblical Spirituality." *Interpretation* 56, no. 2 (2002) 133–42.

———. "Theology and Spirituality: Strangers, Rivals, or Partners?" *Horizons* 13, no. 2 (1986) 253–74.

Schwöbel, Christoph, ed. *Trinitarian Theology Today: Essays on Divine Being and Act*. Edinburgh: T&T Clark, 1995.

Silva, Ken. "Henry Blackaby's Mysticism-Lite Negates Sola Scriptura." *Apprising Ministries*. April 12, 2012. http://apprising.org/2012/04/12/henry-blackabys-mysticism-lite-negates-sola-scriptura/.

Smith, James K. A. *The Fall of Interpretation: Philosophical Foundations for a Creational Hermeneutic*. 2nd ed. Grand Rapids: Baker Academic, 2012.

———. *Thinking in Tongues: Pentecostal Contributions to Christian Philosophy*. Grand Rapids: Eerdmans, 2010.

Smith, Karen E. *Christian Spirituality*. London: SCM, 2007.

Sproul, R. C. "Sola Scriptura: Crucial to Evangelicalism." In *Foundation of Biblical Authority*, edited by James Montgomery Boyce, 103–19. Grand Rapids: Zondervan, 1978.

Stephenson, Christopher A. "The Role of Spirituality and the Rule of Doctrine: A Necessary Relationship in Theological Method." *Journal of Pentecostal Theology* 15, no. 1 (2006) 83–105.

Stetzer, Ed. "Understanding the Charismatic Movement." *The Exchange* (blog). October 18, 2013. http://www.christianitytoday.com/edstetzer/2013/october/charismatic-renewal-movement.html.

Street, et al. *Global Christianity—A Report on the Size and Distribution of the World's Christian Population*. Pew Research Center. December 19, 2011. http://www.pewforum.org/2011/12/19/global-christianity-movements-and-denominations/.

Sundberg, Walter. "Princeton School." In *Dictionary for Theological Interpretation of the Bible*, edited by Kevin J Vanhoozer. Grand Rapids: SPCK, 2005.

Synan, Vinson. *The Holiness-Pentecostal Tradition: Charismatic Movements in the Twentieth Century*. Grand Rapids: Eerdmans, 1997.

Bibliography

Thiselton, Anthony. *The First Epistle to the Corinthians: A Commentary on the Greek Text.* Grand Rapids: Eerdmans, 2000.

Tidball, Derek. "Post-War Evangelical Theology: A Generational Perspective." *Evangelical Quarterly* 81, no. 2 (2009) 145–60.

Tozer, A. W. *The Pursuit of God.* Kindle ed. Abbotsford, WI: Aneko, 2015.

———. *Ten Sermons on the Voices of God Calling Man.* Tozer Pulpit. Harrisburg, PA: Christian Publications, 1981.

Treier, Daniel J. *Introducing Theological Interpretation of Scripture: Recovering a Christian Practice.* Grand Rapids: Baker Academic, 2008.

Turner, Max. "Gifts of the Spirit." In *New Dictionary of Biblical Theology*, edited by T. Desmond Alexander and Brian S. Rosner. Leicester, UK: InterVarsity, 2000.

Twelftree, Graham H. "Signs and Wonders." In *New Dictionary of Biblical Theology*, edited by T. Desmond Alexander and Brian S. Rosner. Leicester, UK: InterVarsity, 2000.

Van Asselt, Willem J. "Protestant Scholasticism: Some Methodological Considerations in the Study of Its Development." *Dutch Review of Church History (Nederlands Archief Voor Kerkgeschiedenis)* 81, no. 3 (2001) 265–74.

Vanhoozer, Kevin J., et al., eds. *Dictionary for Theological Interpretation of the Bible.* Grand Rapids: SPCK, 2005.

———. *The Drama of Doctrine: A Canonical-Linguistic Approach to Christian Theology.* 1st ed. Louisville: Westminster John Knox, 2005.

Van Til, Cornelius. *Christianity and Barthianism.* Philadelphia, PA: Presbyterian & Reformed, 1962.

———. *The New Modernism: An Appraisal of the Theology of Barth and Brunner.* Philadelphia: Presbyterian & Reformed, 1946.

Vinay, Gustavo. "Spiritualità: Invito a Una Discussione." *Studia Medievali* 3a serie 2 (1961) 705–9.

Viola, Frank. "Legalism, License, Lordship and Liberty." *Beyond Evangelical* (blog). April 5, 2011. http://frankviola.org/2011/04/05/legalism-license-lordship-and-liberty/.

Wallace, Daniel B. "The Uneasy Conscience of a Non-Charismatic Evangelical." *Bible. org.* June 30, 2004. http://bible.org/article/uneasy-conscience-non-charismatic-evangelical.

Walton, John H. "Creation in Genesis 1:1–2:3 and the Ancient Near East: Order Out of Disorder After Chaoskampf." *Calvin Theological Journal* 43, no. 1 (2008) 48–63.

Wells, David F. *No Place for Truth; Or, Whatever Happened to Evangelical Theology?* Grand Rapids: Eerdmans, 1993.

Whitney, Donald S. "Defining the Boundaries of Evangelical Spirituality." Paper presented at the 53rd Annual Meeting of the Evangelical Theological Society, Colorado Springs, CO, November 15, 2001.

Wigner, Daniel E. "Clarity in the Midst of Confusion: Defining Mysticism." *Perspectives in Religious Studies* 34, no. 3 (2007) 331–45.

Willard, Dallas. *The Spirit of the Disciplines: Understanding How God Changes Lives.* San Francisco: Harper & Row, 1988.

Wiseman, James A. *Spirituality and Mysticism: A Global View.* Maryknoll, NY: Orbis, 2006.

Yoder, John Howard. *The Politics of Jesus.* Grand Rapids: Eerdmans, 1972.

Zahl, Simeon. *Pneumatology and Theology of the Cross in the Preaching of Christoph Friedrich Blumhardt: The Holy Spirit Between Wittenberg and Azusa Street.* London: T&T Clark, 2010.

Bibliography

Zito, Christopher C. "Mystical Union as Interpretive Community: Ontological Foundations for a New-Creational Hermeneutic of Scripture in Dialogue with James K. A. Smith and John Zizioulas." PhD. diss., Evangelische Theologische Faculteit, 2012.

Index

Alexander, Archibald, 13, 14n12
Augustine, Saint, 62–63, 113
authority
   of Apostles, 89, 105
   of Bible, 25, 28n54, 65, 68, 74
   of divine gifts, 23
   doctrine, 42
   evil spirits, 128
   of Holy Spirit, 123

Barth, Karl, 17n19, 20–21, 51, 74–75
Bible
   encountering God through (*see* encounter), and evangelicalism, 25, 27, 28, 30
   empirical/rationalist reading of, 6n13, 13, 14, 14n12, 15, 28, 42n2, 47–48, 56, 56n29, 56n31, 65–66, 74, 113
   experientialist language in, 43–45, 77
   as genuine means for knowing God spiritually, 3, 58–59
   infallibility of, 21, 22n35, 27, 28, 36, 45, 65n44, 68
   insufficient means of itself for knowing God spiritually, 5, 28, 38–39, 55, 57, 62–64, 74–75
   nature of, 14, 30
   perceived as sufficient means for knowing God spiritually, 3, 13, 43
   pietist principle of reading, 5, 59–62
   reduction of (*see* reductionism)
   situational in character, 66, 68
   spirituality of (*see* spirituality)
   subjective reading, 68
   study of, 13, 18, 28, 39, 43, 50, 56, 59, 60, 64, 73, 75
   as transformative, 60–61, 60n36
   value of, 49
   vs. Spirit, 2, 64
   and word of God (*see* word of God)
bibliolatry
   definition, 45, 55, 63
   epistemological grounding in propositionalism, 45–48
   idolatrous, 48, 110
   legalistic, 65, 70–71, 72, 73
   materialistic/naturalistic view of Bible, 46–48, 61–62, 74
   reductionist, 48, 50, 55, 61, 65, 71
Bloesch, Donald, 25, 28, 41n1, 110n2, 122–23, 122n29, 124, 131
body (physical human), 114, 115, 116, 118, 119, 120, 127, 129, 131

carnality, 37, 62, 68, 78, 79, 85, 86, 87, 88, 90, 93, 106, 126–29, 129n49, 130
charismatic movement, 2, 6, 6n12, 8, 25, 27, 28n55, 31–36, 42, 70, 83n10, 89, 91, 92, 96, 99, 101, 102n33, 127
cross, 6, 6n13, 8, 58, 59, 84, 85, 89, 90, 91–96, 98, 99, 100, 101, 103, 105, 106, 107, 110, 110n3, 122, 132

Index

cross-centered spirituality. *See under* spirituality

Deism, 11–12, 13
disciple/discipleship, 2, 7, 33, 43, 44, 45, 49, 52–53, 58, 60, 66n46, 71, 73, 78, 82, 85, 90–91, 93, 97–99, 103, 105, 130
discipline(s), 56n31, 58n32, 70n51, 71
disobedience, 69, 127, 130
doctrinalism
    and biblioloatry, 42, 43, 57, 63, 65, 66, 69–70, 71–72, 77
    definition, 5
    vs. evangelical spirituality, 6n12
    methodological issues, 7, 8
    vs. experientialism (*see* experientialism)
doctrine, 4, 4n10, 5, 6, 7, 8, 9, 10, 11, 12, 17, 18, 21, 22, 24, 26, 29, 30, 36, 37, 38, 40, 41, 42, 43, 45, 45n7, 48, 48–49n18, 59, 65, 66, 67, 68, 69, 76, 84, 85, 92, 93, 96, 99, 109, 111, 113, 121, 123, 132
dualism, 8, 113–14, 118, 120–21, 122, 123, 127, 129n49

embodied spirituality. *See under* spirituality
encounter, 3, 5, 7, 21, 22, 50, 51, 55, 57, 61, 62, 64, 74, 74n53, 75, 76, 118
enthusiasm, 2, 22, 31, 115, 119, 120, 123
epistemology, 30, 46, 49n18, 57, 64, 65, 67
evangelicalism
    activist, 121
    adherents, 34n71
    contemporary, 7, 8, 12, 81, 83, 84
    definition, 1n1
    doctrinalist, 42, 70, 45, 46, 56, 122
    experientialist, 118
    legalist (*see* bibliolatry)
    reformist, 26, 30
    and spirituality (*see* spirituality)
    Spiritualization of, 1–4, 1n3
    traditional, 3, 6n12, 8, 10, 41, 42, 43
    traditionalist, 26, 28–29, 63

experience
    of Baptism of Spirit, 31
    centrality of, 28
    of Christian perfection, 16
    concupiscent, 131
    of cross, 58
    of dependence on God, 17
    in culture at large, 34–35
    of God, 1, 2, 5, 12, 15, 17, 29, 30, 43, 44, 47–48, 53, 55, 57, 77, 106, 119
    and hermeneutics, 106
    of Holy Spirit, 65, 69, 72, 73, 78, 85, 95, 97
    interpretation of, 85
    of Jesus Christ, 64, 75
    as measure of spirituality, 4, 115, 117
    as measure of truth, 5, 39, 56n31, 106–7
    passive, 119
    of power, 94, 96
    reductionism of (*see* reductionism)
    and Romanticism, 34
    for sake of it, 98
    and spirituality (*see* spirituality)
    as supreme, 24
    of worship, 87
experiences
    authority of, 68
    emotional, 77, 79
    emphasis on, 28
    evaluation of, 3, 42, 106, 131, 132
    of God, 5, 78, 115
    of Holy Spirit, 3, 28, 79, 86–87, 107
    liberating, 2
    limits of, 28
    as measure of spirituality, 88, 89, 131
    physical, 77
    imitation of others', 34, 94, 95, 96, 99, 100–101, 103, 105, 106
    pursuit of, 48, 87
    of the supernatural, 100
    as way of knowing God, 2
    vs. Bible/doctrine, 28, 83–84, 85
experientialism
    aim, 118
    definition, 5–6
    experientialist language in Bible (*see* Bible)

Index

vs. doctrinalism, 5–6, 6n12, 7, 8, 9–40, 41, 70, 110–11, 118, 123
neo-pietist, 122n29
vs. intellect, 3, 5–6, 119
vs. relationship, 42

faith
   as apologetic, 21, 26, 27, 36, 43
   gets answers, 91, 107
   role of Holy Spirit in, 58
   living, 12, 36, 123
   as mental assent, 5, 10, 11, 12, 15, 28, 33, 42, 50, 52, 56, 74, 110
   non-rational dimensions of, 30
   object of, 10
   practical aspect, 123n31
   as personal response, 1
   rationalist, 14, 15, 21, 57, 62n39
   right doctrine as necessary condition for, 5, 17, 27
   seeking understanding, 15
   through hearing, not seeing, 104, 105
   as trust, 10, 103n35
flesh. *See* carnality

gifts, of the Spirit, 22, 23, 28n54, 32, 33, 34n71, 83, 84, 86, 87, 88, 91–96, 97n25, 99, 102, 107, 123, 126

hermeneutics/interpretation, 14n12, 20, 21, 28–29, 30, 46, 50, 51, 56–57, 56n31, 58, 59, 60, 62–63, 68, 75, 76, 85, 103, 106–7, 113, 122, 128
Hodge, Charles, 13, 14, 17
Holiness movement, 16–17, 18n24, 22, 23, 24, 27, 31

idolatry. *See* bibliolatry, pneumatolatry
intellect/mind, 2, 3, 4n6, 5, 11, 13n10, 14, 15, 27, 28, 29, 47, 48, 49–50, 54–62, 63, 68, 72, 73, 74, 75, 79, 115, 119, 120, 121, 130, 132

Kempis, Thomas à, 59–60, 70nn50–51
Keswick, 16, 19, 24, 27n52, 129n49
knowledge

certain, 47
   of Bible/doctrine, 9, 15, 46, 55, 62, 64
   of God, 4, 8, 29, 30, 36, 45, 48, 56, 57, 58, 61, 63, 65, 79
   doctrinal, 5, 7
   experiential, 2, 5, 7
   of God
      hidden, 132
      intellectual, 9
      living, 61
      propositional, 30, 45
      saving, 50, 55
      source of, 5, 11n3
      spiritual, 62, 77, 79, 108, 109, 110
      subjective, 68n48
      true, 15, 36, 46, 47, 48, 55, 61, 63, 65, 79, 110n3
      vs. relationship, 42

legalism. *See* bibliolatry: legalistic
Lloyd-Jones, Martyn, 27n52, 28, 28n55, 29, 70n50
lordship/guidance of Holy Spirit, 8, 44, 61n38, 65–73, 85, 124, 130, 131, 132
Luther, Martin, 3, 10, 12, 58, 65n44, 96, 110n3, 129n49

MacArthur, John, 28n55, 66, 83n10
mysticism, 2, 12, 30, 33n70, 35, 50, 58, 70, 75, 102n31, 102n33, 112–13, 115–16, 118, 119, 122, 123, 132

neo-orthodoxy, 20–22
neo-pietism, 22n35, 28, 41, 66, 113, 122n29
Neoplatonism. *See under* dualism

obedience, 48, 65, 70, 71, 72, 73, 76, 80, 84, 85, 123, 127–28, 129, 130

Pentecostalism, 2n3, 8, 18n24, 20, 22–24, 24n40, 25n44, 27, 31, 32, 33, 34, 35, 36, 83n10, 85, 95, 96, 99, 102n33
personalism, 12, 29

145

Index

Pietism, 8, 11–12, 17, 17n19, 18n24, 22, 41
pietist spirituality. *See under* spirituality
Piper, John, 28, 70n50
pneumatikos, 113, 124–27
pneumatolatry, 6n13, 78–79, 83, 88, 91, 94, 95–96, 99, 110, 119
power
   of age to come, 52, 100
   in experientialist practice and thought, 32–33, 35, 119, 123, 128, 131–32
   of Christ, 107, 108
   to evangelize, 98
   of God, 43, 88, 90, 94, 96, 97, 106
   kingdom, 92, 93, 99
   lack of, 2, 5, 8, 55, 64, 102n34, 104
   manifest, 93, 94, 95, 97, 99, 107, 110
   to perform miracles, 93, 94, 96, 98, 101, 103, 104, 105, 107
   of the Scriptures, 74
   resurrection, 93, 108
   of speech, 89
   of Spirit, 54, 77, 78, 80, 84, 93, 103, 108, 130, 132
   spiritual, 60, 89, 90, 91, 91n18, 97–98
   veiled (of cross), 89, 93, 97, 100, 105, 106, 110
practical spirituality. *See under* spirituality
practice(s), Christian, 2, 3, 7n15, 8, 11, 32, 33, 35, 43, 58, 65, 66, 67, 68, 69, 70, 70n51, 72, 87, 92, 94, 102n33, 110, 114, 115, 119, 123
presence, divine, 1, 2, 3–4, 5–6, 23, 36, 43, 77, 91n18, 114, 118, 119, 120, 123
Princeton, school:, 13–15, 17–18, 56, 57n31
propositionalism, 5, 30, 45–48, 49n18, 57, 61, 64, 72
Puritanism, 11, 12, 27

quietism, 115, 116, 119, 123

rationalism:, 2, 3, 6n13, 7, 10, 11, 12, 13, 14, 15, 17, 21, 28, 29, 30n61, 31, 33, 34, 36, 41, 45, 46, 56n29, 57–58, 63, 73, 102n33, 106, 113, 120, 122n29
reductionism: of Bible, 28–29, 42–43, 45, 47, 48, 59, 61–62
   of experience, 79
   naturalistic, 46n11, 47–48
   of spirituality/knowledge of God, 50, 56, 63–64, 77, 110, 111, 123
   of word of God, 54–55, 56, 57
relationship, with God, 3, 5, 6, 12, 17, 29, 42, 44, 45, 48, 57, 64, 65–66, 66n46, 70, 78, 107, 109, 115, 118, 121, 130
revivalism, 12, 13, 15, 16, 19, 22, 23, 24, 27, 29, 33

sanctification, 15, 31, 32, 44, 71, 92, 97n25, 106, 107, 129n49
scholasticism, method, 5, 10, 12, 13, 14, 19, 20, 21, 22, 24, 26, 27, 29, 30, 31, 41, 56, 65, 110,n3, 113, 114
Scholasticism, Protestant, 8, 11n3, 12, 15n15
scientism, 41, 42n1, 45, 46, 48, 57
Scripture. *See* Bible
signs and wonders, 66n46, 87, 90–91, 93, 94, 96, 98, 101, 102–6
sola scriptura, 27, 65, 70, 71
spirituality
   in Bible, 121–22, 121n25
   of Bible, 62–64
   biblical, 124–32
   bi-polar, 117–18
   cross-centered, 6, 8, 32, 58, 59, 61, 97, 98, 101, 110, 111, 121–32
   doctrinalist, 109–10, 120–21
   conceived of as maturity, 87, 88, 108, 127, 129–30
   embodied, 6, 8, 39, 58–59, 61, 100–106, 121–32
   experiential aspect, 1, 17, 24, 28, 30, 56, 63, 70, 71, 77, 78, 87, 94–95, 103, 109–10, 115, 118, 131
   experientialist, 41–42, 77, 81, 83, 87, 91–92, 93, 96, 97, 110, 118
   evangelical, 6, 7, 109–10, 111, 112–13, 118, 127–32

Index

nature of, 5
practical, 2, 8, 12, 15, 29, 30, 31, 37, 56n29, 58, 80–81, 82, 83, 93, 107, 114, 115, 116, 122, 123, 124, 127–28, 128–29, 132
subjectivity, 5, 6, 8, 14, 17, 34, 46, 68, 68n48, 118

theology, 15n47, 17, 30, 36, 42, 43, 46–48, 56–58, 65
Trinity, 18, 79–83, 84, 86

union/communion with God, 2, 3, 8, 57, 60, 123

Warfield, Benjamin, 13, 14, 18, 19, 22–23
Word of God, 20, 22, 26, 43, 49–54, 55, 56, 59, 60n36, 62n39, 63, 64, 65, 69, 74, 76, 122
worship, 2, 3, 27, 43, 53, 61, 69, 77, 78, 79–87, 90, 91, 93, 97, 99, 119

www.ingramcontent.com/pod-product-compliance
Lightning Source LLC
Chambersburg PA
CBHW071507150426
43191CB00009B/1440